101 Social Media Tactics for Nonprofits

101 Social Media Tactics for Nonprofits

A FIELD GUIDE

Melanie Mathos
Chad Norman

WILEY

John Wiley & Sons, Inc.

Published by John Wiley & Sons, Inc., Hoboken, New Jersey.
Published simultaneously in Canada.

For general information on our other products and services or for technical
support, please contact our Customer Care Department within the United States at
(800) 762-2974, outside the United States at (317) 572-3993, or fax (317) 572-4002.

Wilcy also publishes its books in a variety of electronic formats. Some content that
appears in print may not be available in electronic books. For more information
about Wiley products, visit our web site at www.wiley.com.

Library of Congress Cataloging-in-Publication Data:
Mathos, Melanie, 1979-
    101 social media tactics for nonprofits : a field guide / Melanie Mathos, Chad
Norman.
        p.   cm.
    Includes index.
    ISBN 978-1-118-10624-2 (cloth); ISBN 978-1-118-21887-7 (ebk);
    ISBN 978-1-118-21888-4 (ebk); ISBN 978-1-118-21889-1 (ebk);
    1. Social media.   2. Nonprofit organizations.   I. Norman, Chad, 1973-
II. Title.   III. Title: One hundred and one social media tactics for nonprofits.
HM742.M37 2012
302.23—dc23
                                                                2011039739

Printed in the United States of America
10 9 8 7 6 5 4 3 2 1

We dedicate this book to all the do-gooders out there—the nonprofit professionals who are taking risks, following their hearts, and coming up with some of the most unique, inspiring, and authentic social media communications anywhere.

Contents

Foreword

I have spent the last 32 years working in, for, and with nonprofit organizations. Most of that time has been spent helping nonprofits think about strategy as well as the mindset changes and skills required to embrace new online technologies to support their mission-driven work. As I witnessed the birth of the World Wide Web in 1992 and later Web 2.0, nonprofits often face challenges adopting new tools because it requires taking the time to acquire and internalize new skills.

When I started blogging in 2003, blogs and nonprofit social media use were only in their infancy and nonprofit leaders typically viewed them with a high degree of skepticism about their value. This was one of the main reasons I wrote the book *The Networked Nonprofit* with Alison Fine because I wanted to help the millions of staff people and board members of nonprofit organizations, get over the fear of change and make their way into this new, social world.

The Networked Nonprofit was aimed at helping nonprofit leaders take those first steps to be successful managing social change today in an age of connectedness and to pave the way for organizational adoption. It walked nonprofit leaders through the process of transitioning their thinking and orientation from managing organizations to participating in and managing social networks. But that is only halfway down the path to successful outcomes.

In my role as Visiting Scholar at the David and Lucile Packard Foundation where I am studying the interaction of social media, networks, and nonprofits, I have the honor of working with scores of nonprofits who no longer question whether or not to embrace social media and online networks, but how to do it effectively.

My capacity building, coaching, and training work with nonprofits uses a "Ready, Set, Go" framework. The "Ready and Set" involves identifying who they want to reach, articulating clear and measurable results, and an integrated communications strategy. The "Go" is the implementation where I provide coaching and time-saving tips—much like the nuggets provided in this book. Putting a new way of working into practice can be difficult, but having practical, time-saving tips can make all the difference in the world.

I know how difficult it is to make the leap into effective practice with a new technology tool. In 1992, the New York Foundation for the Arts hired me to serve as the network weaver for ArtsWire, an online network of arts organizations and artists. ArtsWire was an online community that allowed both artists and arts administrators to use the Internet to connect with one another, but also learn how to use online communications technology to support their missions.

As the Internet became more mainstreamed, my job changed dramatically—from providing ongoing technical support in using the online community platform to providing training in strategic online technology plans. As the World Wide Web opened up the possibility for any nonprofit to have a web presence and use e-mail instead of fax machines, I was also responsible for designing and delivering trainings to nonprofits on these topics. I taught hundreds of workshops to thousands of arts organizations to help them establish their very first web site, use e-mail to connect with supporters, take the first foray into online fundraising, or how to use search to find information online.

When I started the work, I didn't know a modem from a microwave. While I was lucky enough to be given a front row seat in the creation of a new field for nonprofits—using the Internet to increase the impact of their work, I was not a natural-born techie. I had the passion to learn, but when I taught myself I would often fail and it would result in hours of wasted time. What helped me was working side by side with a small group of Internet geeks who generously and patiently showed me all the shortcuts and shared tips that helped me be more effective helping nonprofits to embrace the Internet.

This book, *101 Social Media Tactics for Nonprofits*, is like having two very tolerant and technologically savvy friends sit down with you and share their wisdom and experience about social media tactics. Melanie Mathos and Chad Norman have patiently and generously shared their best time-saving tips to help your nonprofit get to the "go" of using social media channels quickly and successfully.

BETH KANTER

Author, Beth's Blog (www.bethkanter.org)

Co-Author, *The Networked Nonprofit*

Acknowledgments

I want to thank my husband, parents, sister, and all of my family for their unwavering support of all that I do. Dating all the way back to third grade when my parents let me take computer programming classes for fun, to my sophomore year in college when my mom subtly suggested that I may want to declare a major at some point (which turned out to be journalism), they helped me become me.

I also want send a special thanks out to my writing/geek muses: my Aunt Janice J. Apostolou, a poet and shining light; my husband, Gary Mathos, who makes sure I hear about the latest tech news and am in on the beta; my friend and the co-author of this book, Chad Norman, who conquers fun projects like this with me and helps me explore my inner geek; and all of the many people with whom I've had the pleasure of volunteering. Most of all, I am eternally grateful to my sweet daughter Elyse, who was such a good baby during many, many phone interviews.

MELANIE MATHOS

They say the nerd doesn't fall far from the tree, so I first want to thank my parents for teaching me to love tech. They encouraged me to creatively explore technology through programming, photography, and publishing—they loved it when I made stuff. Then there's my best friend and wife Jennifer, who has always led me out into the waves. I couldn't have finished this project without her daily support, encouragement, and inspiration. But I'm most thankful for my greatest creations of all time, Cooper, Graham, and Zoe, who keep me motivated to not only do good, but to do it all.

I also ned to give a shout out to Mary Colson, George Huffman, Kevin Swan, Raymond Minnis, and Steve MacLaughlin for putting me on the right path at the right time. And a million thanks to my friend and co-author Melanie Mathos. I'm glad our lives will forever be linked by our nptech geekery and willingness to take on insane challenges like writing this book.

CHAD NORMAN

Introduction

There are a lot of books about social media strategy—this isn't one of them! *101 Social Media Tactics for Nonprofits* features 101 actionable tactics that anyone managing or supporting a social media program for nonprofits can start using today—and most of the featured resources are free.

First, before you go any further, we're assuming you have a social media strategy in place . . . right? Experimenting with social media is fun and exciting (and can be a great way to kill some time), but it's key to start with a well thought-out plan that supports your organization's overall marketing, communications—and yes—even your fundraising strategy. (We know, we know, it's hard to imagine a day when development and marketing actually work together, but it is happening right now as we speak at some of the nation's most successful nonprofits!)

So where do the tactics fit in? Borrowing from the POST method (a systematic approach to social strategy from *Groundswell* authors Charlene Li and Josh Bernoff),[1] in its most simple form, a social strategy should consist of a four- step approach:

1. **P**eople—Where are your constituents engaging and how can you best reach them?
2. **O**bjectives—What do you want to accomplish?
3. **S**trategy—What do you want things to look like when you're done?
4. **T**echnology—How are you going to get there?

---

[1]Josh Bernoff, "The POST Method: A Systematic approach to social strategy," December 11, 2007, http://forrester.typepad.com/groundswell/2007/12/the-post-method.html.

Tactics fit in nicely with technology—and that's where we are fast-forwarding to with *101 Social Media Tactics for Nonprofits*. If you haven't conquered the first three steps, don't cheat! Find your people, determine your objectives, and create your strategy, and then when you are ready to dive in, pick up your trusty field guide, and get to work.

Using This Book

Each of the 101 tactics are numbered and broken down into five key areas: Setup, Communicate, Engage, Fundraise, and Measure. Each tactic will explain the steps and tools needed to implement it, and many are accompanied by a real-life example of a nonprofit using the tactic. You'll read how leading nonprofit professionals around the world are leveraging social media to engage constituents, communicate their causes, and deliver on their missions.

If you have a strategy in place, you can use the Tactic Checklist to find social media ideas that meet your goals. It's like a formula—pick a desired outcome then choose the tactics needed to make it happen. The numbers make it easy to flip through this field guide and find the tactics you need. Here are three examples of strategic outcomes and the tactics that can help make them a reality:

- Connect with your local community: 3, 4, 21, 22, 25, 60, 61, and 86
- Raise more money for your organization: 77 through 90
- Increase traffic to your organization's web site: 11, 14, 23, 26, 28, 32, 38, 44, 48, 93, and 94

These groups of tactics will form the framework of your plan, giving you a method to your social media madness. Read about each tactic you have identified, decide if it will help you meet your goals, and get started.

As you work your way through the field guide, you too will be able to make an immediate impact on your organization's social presence and engage with supporters in new and inventive ways. Pretty soon, you'll be a social media guide, serving as a mentor to up-and-coming social-medialites!

The learning never stops. Visit our web site, 101socialmediatactics. com for online resources and additional tactics.

Tactic Checklist

Setup

- ❏ 1. Claim Your User Name on Facebook
- ❏ 2. Brand Your YouTube Channel
- ❏ 3. Claim Your Venue on foursquare
- ❏ 4. Create a Branded foursquare Page
- ❏ 5. Create a Custom Twitter Background
- ❏ 6. Brand Your Facebook Page
- ❏ 7. Add Multiple Administrators to Your Facebook Page
- ❏ 8. Set and Display Rules for Your Facebook Community
- ❏ 9. Allow Supporters to Post Content on Your Facebook Page
- ❏ 10. Monitor Facebook Page Activity with Alerts
- ❏ 11. Use Commenting Tools that Authenticate with Social Accounts
- ❏ 12. Add a Facebook Like Button to Your Web Site or Blog
- ❏ 13. Add a Twitter Follow Button to Your Site
- ❏ 14. Include the ShareThis Sharing Button
- ❏ 15. Create a Flickr Pro Account
- ❏ 16. Publish Photos Under a Creative Commons License
- ❏ 17. Submit Your Photos to Flickr Groups

Communicate

- ❏ 18. Use Collaboration Tools to Manage Twitter Accounts
- ❏ 19. Create Twitter Lists
- ❏ 20. Display Names of Staff Contributing to Twitter and Facebook
- ❏ 21. Connect with the Top Tweeters in Your Area
- ❏ 22. Monitor Local Twitter Activity Using Hashtags
- ❏ 23. Make Your Tweets Retweetable
- ❏ 24. Sign up for Tweets for Good
- ❏ 25. Recruit New Staff and Volunteers
- ❏ 26. Start, Join, and Organize Conversations with Hashtags
- ❏ 27. Promote an Event or Campaign with a Hashtag
- ❏ 28. Contribute to Mission-Related Hashtags
- ❏ 29. Use TwitPic to Share Photos and Videos
- ❏ 30. Display RSS Feeds on Your Web Site
- ❏ 31. Display Live Twitter Content on Your Web Site and Blog
- ❏ 32. Feed Your Blog to Twitter and Facebook
- ❏ 33. Use Facebook Social Plugins on Your Site

Engage

1

Setup

The beginning of every social media journey is an exciting time, whether you've been tasked with creating a program from scratch or adding a new twist to an existing one. The low barrier to entry of social platforms means nonprofits can begin engaging their supporters right away, so making sure things are in order from the start can make a big difference.

Before you take your organization and supporters on this journey, it's important to get things set up properly. In a perfect world, you'll already have a strategy in place, a social media policy rolled out to your staff, and all of your accounts created and beautifully branded. Since that isn't always the case, it's always a good idea to look at how other nonprofits have setup their programs.

Tactics like branding your Twitter page, setting up your Facebook uniform resource locator (URL), integrating social media into your web site, and other topics covered in this chapter will ensure a better social experience for your supporters and make life easier for your organization. Think of these setup tasks as the first few steps on the journey—steps you need to take in order to reach your final destination.

Even if you've already started the journey, it's always a good idea to look back, review, and refine the social experience you're providing. Sometimes a nonprofit will start a social program simply because someone told them they needed to, and this can lead to wrong turns. This chapter will help you stay on track and get the most out of your social media efforts.

Are you ready to begin? Let's go. . .

Claim Your User Name on Facebook

Creating a unique user name allows you to promote your Facebook presence via a short URL. Instead of saying "find us on Facebook," you can provide potential supporters with a link that leads them directly to your page. This comes in especially handy in conversations and print marketing materials. With the ever-expanding world of Facebook, be sure to grab your unique URL as soon as possible, before someone else does!

What You Need   A Facebook page with at least 25 likes

How to Do It

1. Visit facebook.com/username.
2. From the interface, choose which page you would like to select a user name for.
3. If your desired name is not available, try and try again— maybe an acronym will work instead!

A Closer Look   Things you should know about Facebook user names:

- Make it easy to remember. Think clear, descriptive, and simple when selecting your user name. If you have a Twitter account, you should consider using the same handle. If your organization's name is long, you may want to use an acronym (if it is easily recognizable.) Generic words like "flowers" or "pizza" are not available for use at this time.
- Make sure you are 100 percent positive that the name you choose is the name you want forever before you click "Confirm." Changing your Facebook user name once submitted is not an option, even if you misspelled it.
- Usernames are not transferable. This is a good thing! It protects Facebook from the creation of fake accounts and protects users from "squatters" who are merely setting up an account to claim a name and retain it for future use or sale.
- Facebook has a process for protecting intellectual property rights. If you go to select your user name and it is already taken, the only protection you have is if you are the legal

trademark owner for the term. Facebook offers a user-name intellectual property-infringement form that you must fill out to reclaim your name.

 Brand Your YouTube Channel

If your nonprofit is using YouTube to host videos and engage supporters, taking the time to brand your organization's channel should be part of the plan. You may be posting your videos on Facebook or your blog, but people will still be visiting your YouTube channel. That's why it's so important to have your organization's brand well represented. YouTube offers additional branding options through its Nonprofit Program that can turn your channel into a great destination.

What You Need   A YouTube account, a YouTube Nonprofit Program membership, and someone to design your graphics

How to Do It
1. Create a YouTube account for your organization if you haven't already done so.
2. Apply for YouTube's Nonprofit Program by visiting www .youtube.com/nonprofits, and pressing the "Apply" button.
3. Determine the overall look and feel of your YouTube channel, including incorporating your organization's branding, colors, and so on.
4. Design the header, avatar, and background.
5. Go to "Channel Design" and change the colors and modules you want to use on your channel.
6. Access the "Branding Options" section of your channel and upload your icons and banners.

A Closer Look   A well-branded YouTube channel can be an important social media outpost for your organization, so take the opportunity to make it look as professional as possible. The YouTube Nonprofit Program provides many benefits, several of which involve branding and design.

Once your YouTube channel has been accepted into the Nonprofit Program, you can begin customizing your channel. YouTube's Channel Design section will help you set the colors and styles of your channel, which should match your organization's web site and branding standards as closely as possible. You can then upload custom icons, backgrounds, and banners to complete the design.

Because there are so many ways you can customize your YouTube channel, be sure to look around at what other nonprofits have done. Imitation is the sincerest form of flattery, right? Here are four nonprofits that have well-branded YouTube channels that you should check out:

- United Way Worldwide has a really solid, great-looking channel. It features a header linking to its web site, perfectly matched styles, and a great youth-focused background image. www .youtube.com/unitedwaypsas
- Boys and Girls Clubs of America takes a simple approach with its channel, featuring a design that matches its web site. A current campaign is featured in the header, which is a great way to encourage supporters to take action. www .youtube.com/bgcastaff
- The Nature Conservancy has a well-branded header on its channel, which also contains two HTML buttons called "How You Can Help" and "About Us." A Google Checkout donation option is also included near the bottom of the channel, which is another great benefit of YouTube's Nonprofit Program. www.youtube.com/natureconservancy
- America Jewish World Service has done a great job combining a custom header with the background graphic to create a seamless design. The organization also uses a second banner in the left column to drive traffic back to its web site. www .youtube.com/ajwstv

In the end, you just need to strike a balance between being creative and professional. And while creating a great-looking channel is important, don't overlook producing compelling videos that people actually want to watch (see Tactic 41).

3   Claim Your Venue on foursquare

Claiming your venue on foursquare is easy to do, and the reason for doing it is just as simple—to become the "manager" of the venue. Once you claim your venue, foursquare offers organizations a free set of tools to help attract and retain supporters. By becoming the manager, you will be able to edit venue information, including name and address, and will also have access to analytics and offer specials. The approval process generally takes 7 to 10 days and is relatively painless. (If you don't have a physical location, see Tactic 4.)

What You Need   A foursquare account and a physical venue

How to Do It
1. Log in to foursquare. *It is a best practice to create a separate business account to link to a venue as manager information is public.*
2. Search for your venue.
3. In the upper right-hand corner, you will see "Do you manage this venue? Claim here."
4. Click "Claim here" and complete a simple series of questions.

A Closer Look   Social media staffers at The Taft Museum of Art claimed their venue on foursquare to learn more about who was coming and going from the museum (see Exhibit 1.1). According to Tricia Suit, the Museum's marketing and communications manager, the process was simple. And, since it was free to do, they didn't have to cut through any institutional red tape to do it. "I think the hardest part was trying to develop the 'offer'," says Tricia, "imagining what people would want and how they could achieve it." (For more on offers, see Tactic 61.)

Foursquare provides Museum staff with a new way to interact with visitors. Since foursquare is integrated with the organization's Twitter account, staff members are able to track when people are at the Museum and offer them specials in real time. "I noticed on Twitter a guest had checked in and was at the café," says Tricia. "I told her to tell the chef that Tricia said to give her a

The Taft Museum of Art (www.taftmuseum.org) welcomes people of every background to experience a world-renowned collection of Anna and Charles Taft's treasures in a beautiful historic house.

Exhibit 1.1 Taft Museum of Art's foursquare page

Source: Courtesy of the Taft Museum of Art; © 2011, Foursquare Labs, Inc. All of the foursquare® logos and trademarks displayed in these screenshots are the property of Foursquare Labs, Inc.

free iced tea. Through foursquare, I was able to have a conversation with her and help create a unique visitor experience, not just a virtual one."

4 Create a Branded foursquare Page

Foursquare gives you the ability to create a custom page that will serve as a foursquare homepage for your nonprofit's brand. This page allows your organization to customize the look and feel, add tips for followers, share links to key resources, and create a custom URL. The ability to leave tips is very useful because you can leave notes for your followers that engage them in the real world, which is great for advocacy-based nonprofits! If you plan on using foursquare in your social media plans, creating a branded page is a great way to build up your community.

What You Need   A foursquare account, a Twitter account, artwork, and a graphic designer for layout

How to Do It
1. Create a foursquare account for your nonprofit if you don't already have one. This needs to be the same name you used on Twitter (e.g., twitter.com/yourorg and foursquare.com/yourorg). You cannot request a foursquare name that you do not have on Twitter.
2. Create a header image for your foursquare page. It must be 860 × 130, less than 200KB, have a transparent background, and include a foursquare logo.
3. Create a page gallery image. This is to represent your page in the gallery, and must by 185 × 185 and less than 200KB.
4. Visit www.foursquare.com/business and click "Brands."
5. Click "Create a Page," and fill out the form.
6. Wait for confirmation that your page has been created, which can take a couple of weeks.
7. Begin adding tips for your followers.

A Closer Look   The National Wildlife Federation (NWF) does a fantastic job of reaching out to supporters no matter where they are. This drive to engage supporters out in the real world extends to foursquare, where NWF has built a branded page (see Exhibit 1.2). When asked how this effort began, Danielle Brigida, manager of social media at NWF, says, "I was really hoping to provide direct ways to connect people with nature while it was most relevant to them, and that is why we created the branded page of wildlife watching tips. The more we can connect with an audience that is actually out in nature, the better."

When you visit the NWF foursquare page, you'll notice the custom banner right away. The logo and imagery in the header creates continuity with NWF's web site and gives loyal supporters confirmation

The National Wildlife Federation (www.nwf.org) is inspiring Americans to protect wildlife for their children's future.

Exhibit 1.2   National Wildlife Federation's foursquare page

Source: Courtesy of the National Wildlife Federation; © 2011, Foursquare Labs, Inc. All of the foursquare®
logos and trademarks displayed in these screenshots are the property of Foursquare Labs, Inc.

that they are in the right place. The branding also continues on the
right, where NWF has included links to its web site, Facebook page,
and Twitter profile.

In the Tips section of this page, you can see what NWF is really
doing with its foursquare presence. Staff members know that
supporters love wildlife and are often visiting outdoor attractions,
so they have left tips at hundreds of locations around the world.
When supporters check in at these locations, they will receive a
tip relating back to NWF's mission. This could be a reminder of
a great bird-watching spot nearby, or simply pointing out a local
hiking trail.

"Whenever I'm investigating a new tool, I make sure to consider
the time, functionality, and the organizational goal I'm addressing,"
Danielle says. "In this case, the time it would take to create a foursquare page and upload tips seemed very reasonable, and I was also
connecting people to nature in a fun, new way."

The benefit to NWF supporters is clear—more wildlife tips
when and where they need them! Location-based services like

foursquare are making social marketing more real time every day, and for some nonprofits, this can be a great tool for awareness.

 ## Create a Custom Twitter Background

One of the best things about Twitter is that you can use your organization's profile, not just its avatar, to tell a story. Twitter allows users to select either a pre-designed theme or customize their profiles with a unique color scheme and background image. The background of your page essentially becomes your organization's billboard. Consistency is key here—by tying in your Twitter presence with your organization's brand story, it will simply serve as another channel supporting your overall web presence.

What You Need   A Twitter account, artwork, and a graphic designer for layout

How to Do It

1. Create a Twitter background that reflects your organization's brand, incorporating brand colors, strong images that portray what you do, and a call to action (i.e., sign up to volunteer at Mynonprofit.org.)
2. From a technical design perspective, it is best to design up to a 1600 × 1200 pixel image at 72 dpi that is no larger than 800KB. (Experiment with what works.) Be sure to focus your graphics on the left side of the image (you have about 200 pixels on that side to work with.)
3. Log in to Twitter and navigate to "Settings" from the upper right-hand drop-down menu.
4. Click on "Design" and select "Change Background Image."
5. Click "Choose File," select the file from your computer, and click "Save Changes."

A Closer Look   Highveld Horse Care Unit's Twitter profile (twitter. com/hhcu) is a great example of a simple, elegant, and effective branding application on Twitter (see Exhibit 1.3). One visit to the organization's profile and you will not only quickly understand what it does, but also what its staff wants you to do. The mission is clearly

Exhibit 1.3   Highveld Horse Care Unit's Twitter page
Source: Courtesy of the Highveld Horse Care Unit; Twitter

stated in the profile section, and the custom background helps visitors relate to the mission.

The design reflects the organization's brand color palette. The logo is used as an avatar and in the sidebar. Although the organization primarily deals with animal cruelty, the designer chose an uplifting photo that portrayed the brand reward—healthy horses. The design also incorporates a bit of whimsy with a horse walking off the right side of the screen.

Although it is great to engage and interact on Twitter, it is also a best practice to lead people to where they can learn more—your organization's web site. HCCU does a great job of providing a clear call to action for its Twitter visitors. On the left side of the screen,

The Highveld Horse Care Unit (HCCU; www.horsecare.org.za) is the largest equine welfare organization in the Southern hemisphere.

visitors are presented with the organization's web site and are encouraged to "Sign Up, Log On, and Help."

 ## Brand Your Facebook Page

Often, your Facebook page provides the first impression for new supporters, so it's important that your organization's brand is visually represented by more than just its logo. On Facebook, you can use a tall profile picture to display more branding and messaging on your page, such as photos or program callouts. Creative use of the photo strip and custom tab design can really bring your Facebook page together visually and align it better with your other web channels.

What You Need A Facebook page, photos, artwork, logo, and a graphic designer for layout

How to Do It To visually brand your organization's Facebook page, you will need to:

1. Use an image editor or graphic designer to create a Facebook profile picture that includes visual branding elements, such as your organization's logo, color, tagline, photos, and other imagery. While you can use the maximum size of 180 pixels × 540 pixels, keep in mind that you don't want to push your page's navigation too far down the page by making a really tall image.
2. Upload this image to Facebook by pressing the "Edit Page" and clicking on the "Profile Picture" link. Here, you can browse to your new image and upload it.
3. Set the Profile Thumbnail to display part of the image that will look good as a square icon, such as your logo. You can do this by clicking the "Edit Thumbnail" link directly under your uploaded profile picture on the Profile Picture screen.
4. Make sure the photos in your page's photo strip reflect your brand and mission. If you see a photo you don't like, simply hover over it and press the X button. This will remove it from the rotation.
5. Create custom tab content that visually reflects your brand.

A Closer Look   The Foundation for Jewish Camp is a great example of an organization doing more with its Facebook profile picture than simply uploading its logo. In fact, the organization doesn't use its logo at all!

During early 2011, the Foundation's Facebook profile picture featured the logo of its One Happy Camper program, along with supporting photos (see Exhibit 1.4). Joelle Berman, communications manager at the Foundation, says, "Our One Happy Camper program takes center stage on our Facebook page in order to attract our largest target audience: parents (and mainly mothers) who have not yet sent their children to Jewish camp."

> The Foundation for Jewish Camp (www.jewishcamp.org) unifies and galvanizes the field of Jewish overnight camp and significantly increases the number of children participating in transformative summers at Jewish camp, assuring a vibrant North American Jewish community.

Exhibit 1.4   The Foundation for Jewish Camp's Facebook page
Source: Courtesy of The Foundation for Jewish Camp; Facebook

The organization has also continued that design on the One Happy Camper custom tab, where the visual continuity goes from profile picture to page content. Regarding this continuity, Joelle says, "By creating a custom landing page, a custom profile picture, and a custom tab that mirrors our web portal for the program, we are able to make the Facebook experience and the program enrollment experience seamless."

You can take this even further by creating custom tab icons that match your brand, tying in your profile picture with your five featured photos, and by making sure your avatar (the little icon that appears by your posts in people's news feeds) looks great.

 Add Multiple Administrators to Your Facebook Page

You want to make sure your organization's Facebook page has multiple administrators (admins) for the same reason a hotel gives you two keys when you check in: In case you lose one! Having more than one admin protects you from the perils of a key staff member going on vacation, leaving the organization, getting hit by the proverbial bus, or having his or her personal profile suspended (and your page along with it). It also allows you to spread the workload around by providing access to other stakeholders, and lets you give credit to admins on your page.

What You Need   A Facebook page and more than one administrator

How to Do It
1. Find a co-worker or two who want to be administrators on your Facebook page, or at least serve as a backup for you.
2. Visit your organization's Facebook page and press the "Edit Page" button in the upper right, then access the "Manage Admins" section.
3. Enter a Facebook user's name or e-mail address in the blank field, which should be directly under your name and profile picture. If you are not Facebook friends with the person you are trying to add, you will need to enter his or her e-mail address.

4. Add as many admins as you need, then press the "Save Changes" button.
5. Display your admins on your Facebook page by clicking on the "Featured" link, and clicking the "Add Featured Page Admins" button.
6. Train your admins on Facebook best practices and how their new status changes how they can interact with Facebook.

A Closer Look At most nonprofits, the social media program was started by one staff member because he or she was passionate about engaging the community. As social media programs grow and other staff members become involved, the need to manage access to each social media account grows as well.

Why should you have multiple admins?

- To share the workload. If you have a very active Facebook community, it will take a lot of time and energy to keep up with the comments and other activity. Using multiple admins will lighten the workload.
- In case you lose your admin. It's no fun to plan for things like this, but if your only admin leaves the organization, gets fired, or has his or her personal account suspended on Facebook, you may lose access to your Facebook page.
- You have different roles for different admins. As the manager of your social media program, you may be focused more on branding, ads, and metrics, leaving the day-to-day activity to another team member.
- You serve multiple time zones. If your organization's supporters span the country or even the globe, you need to ensure that someone is monitoring the Facebook page as often as possible. Having admins in different time zones will help keep you covered.

8 Set and Display Rules for Your Facebook Community

Having an open community is a great way to create dialogue around your mission and bring your supporters closer together. However, that low barrier to entry can also invite trouble—especially if your organization is controversial in any way. When setting up your Facebook page, it's a good idea to include the rules of your community and outline your commenting policy on the Info tab. By making this information accessible to each visitor, you can nip most cases of abuse in the bud while setting clear expectations for those that slip through the cracks.

What You Need   A Facebook page

How to Do It

1. Determine what types of behavior and comments you want to cover in your rules. These should include things like profanity, spam, attacks, misinformation, illegal activity, and so on.
2. Create a designated point of contact at your organization for the community to reach out to if there are issues. This can be a staff member, or a special e-mail account can be created (e.g., Facebook@YourOrg.org).
3. Draft the policy using clear and concise language. Remember, this is a commenting policy on a Facebook page, not a long legal document. Keep it short and to the point.
4. Review the policy with internal stakeholders. This group should include appropriate representatives from around the company, as well as someone from your legal team.
5. If possible, review the policy with a small group of your most avid supporters. Gaining the perspective of community members may shed light on an unseen issue with the policy.
6. Roll out the policy onto your Facebook page with an announcement on your wall and provide an e-mail address for people to send questions and feedback.

A Closer Look   The Humane Society of the United States (HSUS) attracts a large, active, and engaged community of supporters to its Facebook page, but also a small opposition that posts unwanted and

The Humane Society (www.humanesociety.org) of the United States seeks a humane and sustainable world for all animals, and is America's mainstream force against cruelty, exploitation and neglect, as well as the most trusted voice extolling the human-animal bond.

Exhibit 1.5   The Humane Society of the United States' Facebook Info tab
Source: Courtesy of The Humane Society of the United States; Facebook

inappropriate content. Over time, the HSUS's social media staffers discovered that moderating a Facebook page took time and effort, especially having to explain why they were removing a comment or post each time.

So instead of discussing their policy on their Facebook page, they decided to simply post it (see Exhibit 1.5). Carie Lewis, director of emerging media for HSUS, says, "Social media opened the doors of two-way, two-sided communication, so we realized we needed some protection. We put together a clear, brief, fair commenting policy that protects us from harm, but not from disagreement."

By posting its commenting policy on the Info tab, HSUS provides new members with clear expectations of how the community works, what type of content is appropriate, and what will happen if the guidelines are ignored. Posting the policy also helped admins, as they no longer had to explain why they were taking an action. If a user was upset, the admin could just point him or her to the policy. This also helped executives buy in to the open nature of the Facebook page.

Carie adds, "In the end, we want our page to be a safe place for members to learn what we're doing and connect with each other. There will always be disagreements, tough questions, and complaints, but this is a place to address those in a timely and transparent way."

The HSUS states that by participating on its Facebook page, visitors are agreeing to the commenting policy. The policy plainly says that content will be removed if it contains profanity, misinformation, spam, off-topic content, personal attacks, violence, or illegal or questionable activities. It further says that the person may be removed from the page if the abuse continues. The organization also provides a special e-mail address to contact if a visitor has questions, which is a nice touch. The full policy can be seen on the Info tab at www.facebook.com/humanesociety.

Allow Supporters to Post Content on Your Facebook Page

A healthy portion of engagement is a key ingredient to any thriving social community. Opening up your Facebook page enables your supporters to post content on your wall and leave comments on your photos and videos. This is critical if you are soliciting feedback, wanting your supporters to interact, or just hoping to be there when someone needs you. Before you jump in the user-generated content pool, remember that opening up may expose your organization's brand to a negative comment from time to time.

What You Need   A Facebook page and a commenting policy

How to Do It
1. On your organization's page, press the "Edit Page" button.
2. On the "Manage Permissions" tab, locate the "Posting Ability" section.
3. Mark each of the checkboxes that correspond to the activity you want your supporters to be able to do. These three activities are: write or post content to the wall, add photos, and add videos.
4. In the "Moderation Blocklist" field, type in the terms you want to prevent users from posting. Think of this as your spam filter.

5. Set the "Profanity Blocklist" as needed.

6. Press the "Save Changes" button.

A Closer Look   Having an open Facebook page isn't the right move for everyone, but if you have a loyal supporter base that likes to engage with your brand, consider allowing the members to contribute to your page. Hearing and seeing your mission from a supporter's point of view can be a wonderful way to introduce new people to your organization, and this is an easy way to get the ball rolling.

On the Lance Armstrong Foundation's LIVESTRONG page, supporters have been allowed to leave wall posts, photos, and videos for years (see Exhibit 1.6). Brooke McMillan, LIVESTRONG's online community evangelist says, "We wanted to create a safe and welcoming place for people to share their cancer stories and ask questions. This helps us disseminate our materials and educate people on how we can help them throughout their cancer journey."

When you visit the organization's page, you don't just see posts from the LIVESTRONG staff. You also see supporters thanking the organization for a job well done and sharing their stories about recovery. You'll see photos posted from various events around the country. And, you'll see people sharing moments in their own lives, like a photo of their yellow LIVESTRONG bracelet against a scenic trail background.

Together, all of this content tells the LIVESTRONG story in a way only social media can—by weaving together a tapestry of mission-related images and words that will hopefully move the next visitor to take an action. Brooke says, "Facebook and other social media platforms have continuously stayed in the top three referring sites to our web site and cancer services. Having an open dialogue has helped us share our mission and allow us to fulfill it." Social media let us all tell our stories, so let your supporters tell theirs!

In the fight against cancer, the Lance Armstrong Foundation (www.livestrong.org) believes that unity is strength, knowledge is power, and attitude is everything. Its mission is to inspire and empower people affected by cancer.

Exhibit 1.6   LIVESTRONG'S Facebook page
Source: Courtesy of LIVESTRONG; Facebook

 ## Monitor Facebook Page Activity with Alerts

Being responsive to the activity on your organization's Facebook page is a lot of work, but it is important if you want to develop an engaged community. The best way to make sure you don't miss a single comment, like, or post is to set up notifications for you and your staff. Facebook can be configured to send page administrators e-mail notifications for certain actions, and third-party tools can be used to provide real-time updates of page activity. These alerts help you stay on top of your Facebook page's activity and respond in a timely manner without having to monitor your page all day long.

What You Need   A Facebook page and an e-mail account

How to Do It

1. Access your organization's Facebook page and press the "Edit Page" button.

2. Click the "Your Settings" link in the left navigation.
3. In the "E-mail Notifications" sections, mark the "Send notifications to (your e-mail) when people post or comment on your page" checkbox.
4. Press the "Save Changes" button.
5. To receive weekly page updates via e-mail, you can:
   • Start on the screen from step three above.
   • Click the "View all e-mail settings for your pages" link.
   • Scroll down to the Pages section, and mark the "Weekly Page updates for admins" checkbox.
   • Scroll to the bottom and press the "Save Changes" button.

A Closer Look   The easiest way to get Facebook notifications is via e-mail, which will send you an update each time someone leaves a post or comment on your organization's page. If your organization is using Facebook Events, e-mail notifications can also be turned on to monitor activity on those pages as well (this can be done via the "Notifications" tab in your account settings).

Weekly page updates provide a snapshot of activity over the past week, including number of active users, number of wall posts and comments, and total visits. These e-mails are really just summaries of your Facebook Insights data, but are still useful if you don't actually view your user data on a regular basis, which is something you should be doing (see Tactic 91).

Using social media management tools is a natural evolution at any organization, whether it's moving from an iGoogle dashboard to Radian6, or switching from posting on Twitter.com to scheduling in CoTweet. Facebook management tools can be very beneficial if you're busy and need to schedule updates, but also if you feel the need to monitor your pages activity in real time.

If you're looking for something more robust than e-mail notification, companies like MediaFeedia.com do real-time Facebook monitoring. MediaFeedia will send you real-time updates as people leave comments and posts on your page. You can view the comment in your e-mail, which easily links back to Facebook if you want to reply (and you should, but that's a whole other tactic!). If your social strategy calls for you to be quick to respond when your supporters reach out, these alerts can really help.

Use Commenting Tools that Authenticate with Social Accounts

Creating discussions around your organization's best blog and web site content is an effective way for your supporters to feel more involved with your mission, provide feedback, and engage as a community. Commenting tools that allow users to log in with their social media credentials (e.g., Facebook, Twitter, LinkedIn, etc.) make it much easier for people to participate in a discussion. Commenting systems like Disqus can be used in place of the native functionality in platforms like WordPress, or be used to add comments to systems without them.

What You Need   A web site or blog, access to these files, a commenting tool that supports social media log-ins. *We recommend the Disqus commenting system and will use it as the example moving forward.*

How to Do It
1. Determine what content you would like your supporters to comment on. A blog is a natural place, but also look for areas of your web site, press room, and microsites.
2. Create a Disqus account and grab the code snippet to place on your web site.
3. Insert the code snippet into your blog or web site where you would like to see the comments appear, typically near the bottom of the page.
4. Configure the Disqus account to allow users to log in with Facebook, Twitter, OpenID, and so on.

A Closer Look   Using a third-party commenting tool like Disqus can turn your web site and blog content into an opportunity to interact with your supporters. Adding commenting to popular areas of your web site, in addition to your blog, provides new places where your community can engage with you and your mission.

Based out of northeast Ohio, ideastream is a nonprofit organization bringing Public Broadcasting Service (PBS) and National Public Radio (NPR) to the local area. Supporters of PBS and NPR are very loyal and active, so it makes sense to see commenting throughout ideastream's web site. By using Disqus, ideastream allows users to comment on their blog posts, but also to start conversations around their programming, events, and other key content. This is a great way to engage supporters and build community.

One of the key benefits of using Disqus is that it allows users to log in with their social media credentials to leave comments. This makes it really easy for people who want to leave a comment under their own names, but don't want to create a new account at ideastream's web site. ideastream allows users to authenticate with Facebook, Twitter, Yahoo!, Disqus, and several other methods. Disqus also provides additional functionality some native tools may not have, like live threaded discussions and image uploads.

Disqus also allows ideastream to customize the look and feel of the comments through cascading style sheets (CSS), ensuring that it matches the rest of the web site. This lets designers create links that are the proper color and fonts that match the rest of the web site. This is an important step when using any third-party tool, as you want your web site to look like one cohesive platform.

 Add a Facebook Like Button to Your Web Site or Blog

The Facebook "Like" Button provides your supporters one of the easiest ways to connect with your organization and share your content and brand with their friends. Whether it's from a Like Box or a Like Button, the act of pressing Facebook's ubiquitous button can generate a lot of impressions for your nonprofit, because each click shows up in a supporter's news feed for all their friends to see. Connecting your web site and Facebook can be as easy as putting a Like Box on your home page and putting a Like Button on your blog posts.

What You Need   A Facebook page and access to your web site or blog files.

How to Do It
1. Visit developers.facebook.com/docs/plugins/ and click the "Like Button" or "Profile Box" link.
2. Customize the widget and press the "Get Code" button.
3. Insert the code into your web site or blog template.

A Closer Look   Implementing the Facebook Like Box on your web site or blog is as easy as it sounds, and the widget can be put places like your home page, contact page, or in a page gutter. It can also be integrated into a blog template, or any web property that receives a lot of traffic. The Facebook Like Box can be configured to show visitors if their friends have connected with your organization, display recent updates, and connect people via the Like Button.

The Like Button can also be used to promote your best content, like blog posts, campaign pages, and program microsites. Adding a simple Like Button to these pages helps visitors share the content with their networks. Many people remain logged into Facebook, and the button can be set up to show them which of their own friends have already liked the content.

In fact, Facebook tools can be deeply integrated into your web site if you're willing to get your hands dirty. For instance, the Like Button is very easy to install using the iFrame method—you simply select the features you want, press the "Get Code" button, and paste the code on your site. But if you want greater integration between your web site and the Facebook platform, your need to take a look at the XFBML method. XFBML lets users leave an optional comment that posts to Facebook, as well as automatically resizes the Like Button to fit your site. XFBML involves using the JavaScript SDK, so you may need access to a developer to help write the code.

Greenpeace USA uses the Like Button throughout its web site. You can see the button, along with the total number of likes and the names of your friends who have liked the content, at the top of many key pages, such as the organization's "Volunteer" page. Greenpeace USA also implemented the smaller "Box Count" style button on many other pages, as it takes up less real estate and can be mixed in with other social sharing tools. This decision to include the Facebook Like button is helping the organization promote its content, reach new supporters, and achieve its mission.

 Add a Twitter Follow Button to Your Site

Similar to the Facebook Like button, the Twitter Follow Button is designed to "increase engagement and create a lasting connection with your audience." When you see a Twitter Follow Button on a site, you can instantly follow the organization's Twitter account without having to leave the page (if you are logged in). If you are not logged in to Twitter, a box pops up where you can quickly log in without having to leave the page. It's a great way to increase your followers right from your site without having to worry about them wandering off into Twitterland.

What You Need   A Twitter account and a web developer

How to Do It
1. Visit http://twitter.com/about/resources/followbutton.
2. Enter your organization's user name and select what type of background will be used.
3. Select whether you would like your organization's follower count displayed beside the button. (If you have a lot of followers, this may add to the credibility of your account.)
4. Select your preferred language.
5. Preview the button on the right-hand side.
6. Copy and paste the code into the hypertext markup language (HTML) for your web site wherever you want the button to appear.

A Closer Look   With so many widgets, buttons, plug-ins, and boxes available, your web site's design and true purpose could easily get crowded with all of the social elements. So, how do you tastefully incorporate these great tools while maintaining design integrity and aesthetic? The answer is, strategically. Headers and footers are great places to include buttons. Some organizations opt to build a dedicated page to serve as a social media directory. Just remember, your web site is precious real estate—be sure to use space accordingly!

The Twitter Follow Button can easily be added in the footer or sidebar of your web site, but think of all of the other places it can be (selectively) used:

- Alongside a Twitter box
- Blog sidebars
- Top or bottom of blog posts
- On your "About us" page
- Donation confirmation pages
- Press room
- On a custom tab on your Facebook page

Include the ShareThis Sharing Button

You have great content, right? Well, you don't expect it to share itself do you?! The ShareThis Sharing Button makes it easy for visitors to your site or blog to share content on a variety of social networks and directly with each other. Users can add comments when they share, adding their own thoughts on the content, and making it even more relevant for their networks.

What You Need   A web site or blog with shareable content and a web designer

How to Do It

1. Visit Sharethis.com and click "Get the Button."
2. Select the type of site you will be adding the button to (a web site or blog).
3. Choose a button type and style.
4. Register to get the code (it's free!).
5. Paste the code onto your blog or site wherever you want the button to appear.
6. Add the script tag anywhere on the page (ShareThis recommends putting it in the header).

A Closer Look

Who's sharing what?   In June 2011, ShareThis released a study[1] taking a look at the activity of 300 million people a month who share links with a ShareThis button on more than a million web sites. According to the study, sharing now produces an estimated 10 percent of all Internet traffic and 31 percent of referral traffic to sites from search and social web sites. Facebook accounts for the lion's share of sharing with 38 percent of the pie, while e-mail and Twitter come in second and third with 17 and 11 percent. The remaining 34 percent comes from blogs and bookmarking sites, and so on.

Calls to action spur sharing   The Nature Conservancy wrote a blog post on its "Cool Green Science" blog (http://blog.nature.org/) in

---

[1]Erick Schonfeld, "ShareThis Study: Facebook Accounts For 38 Percent Of Sharing Traffic On The Web," June 6, 2011, http://techcrunch.com/2011/06/06/sharethis-facebook-38-percent-traffic.

early 2010 asking readers a simple question—What Should We Call What Nature Provides Us? The simple 72-word post was among the most popular of the year. Besides the slew of comments the post received, readers shared it with their social networks via a series of social buttons, including the ShareThis Sharing Button. The organization chose to provide a variety of sharing options that resulted in more than 400 total shares of the post.

  Create a Flickr Pro Account

Flickr is a powerful photo platform for storing, sorting, searching, and sharing your organization's photos online. With a free Flickr account, users can upload two videos and 300MB worth of photos each calendar month. Through a program called "Flickr for Good," for a small fee, nonprofits can upgrade to a Flickr "pro" account and enjoy unlimited uploads, storage, bandwidth, sets and collections, access to original files, stats on the account (see Exhibit 1.7), ad-free browsing and sharing, and high definition (HD) video playback.

What You Need   Photos or videos showcasing your organization's work and as little as $6

How to Do It

1. To participate in the Flickr donation program, apply for a nonprofit pro account at Flickr.com/good with either TechSoup (for U.S.- or Canada-based nonprofits) or one of the international partners on the site.
2. Select a package. Pro accounts are available in two or five-packs and range from a $6 admin fee to a $15 admin fee. (The regular rate for a pro account is $24.95 per year.)[2]

A Closer Look

ReSurge International (www.resurge.org; formerly Interplast) provides free reconstructive surgeries for the poor and builds year-round medical access in underserved areas.

---

[2]"Flickr for Good," www.flickr.com/good.

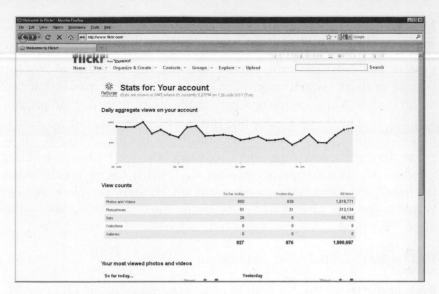

Exhibit 1.7   ReSurge's Flickr Stats page

Source: Courtesy of ReSurge International; Reproduced with permission of Yahoo! Inc. ©2011 Yahoo! Inc. Flickr and the Flickr logo are registered trademarks of Yahoo! Inc.

An early adopter, ReSurge International joined Flickr in 2005 and has built a very active pro account with more than 10,000 photos. A participant in the Flickr for Good program, the organization uses photos to share its story. Through photos, staff can share how the organization is changing people's lives in very dramatic and immediate ways, connecting supporters to their work.

According to Sara Anderson, ReSurge International's chief communications and advocacy officer, when the organization first joined Flickr, staff had two goals in mind: Organize the photos and use the platform for social networking.

The organizational features (sets and tags) have helped ReSurge International clearly sort thousands of photos, making it easier for supporters and staff to find exactly what they're looking for. In addition, Flickr's social properties have made it easy for the organization to integrate photo feeds into other social properties like Facebook, blogs, and even a planned iPhone application.

"Flickr for Good is a wonderful program," says Sara. "We've been very happy with Flickr and their acknowledgement that the nonprofit sector is important—we're pleased they're supporting it."

16   Publish Photos Under a Creative Commons License

One of the most powerful forces in social media is the ability for people to share content easily. For causes, providing media that can be shared by your supporters can really help extend your organization's reach. If you're sharing photos of your mission on Flickr, consider giving them a Creative Commons license. This will allow press, bloggers, and supporters to easily use your photos without needing to obtain your permission first. With Creative Commons licensing, you can customize the copyright to allow people to re-post your images, or alter and remix them into something new—the choice is yours!

What You Need   A Flickr account and some photos

How to Do It   To set your default license to be more open, you can:

1. Create a Flickr account if you do not already have one.
2. Access your Account Settings, and select the "Privacy & Permissions" tab.
3. In the "Defaults for new uploads" section, click the "edit" link next to the "What license will your content have" option.
4. Select the type of Creative Commons license you would like to use, and press the "Set Default License" button.
5. Upload your photos.

To license photos you've already uploaded to Flickr, you can:

• Click the "Organize and Create" link.
• Select the photos for which you want to change the license.
• Select "Change licensing" from the "Permissions" drop-down list.
• Select the Creative Commons license you wish to use, and press the "Change License" button.

A Closer Look   After the 2009 typhoon season in the Philippines, The International Federation of Red Cross and Red Crescent Societies (IFRC) put photos of their relief work up on Flickr (see Exhibit 1.8). Amy Greber, the social media officer at IFRC, says, "Our goal was to extend our photos' reach along with the important message they conveyed. We chose to use Creative Commons licenses as a

Exhibit 1.8   The International Federation of Red Cross and Red Crescent Societies' Flickr photo page

Source: Courtesy of The International Federation of Red Cross and Red Crescent Societies; Reproduced with permission of Yahoo! Inc. ©2011 Yahoo! Inc. Flickr and the Flickr logo are registered trademarks of Yahoo! Inc.

> The International Federation of Red Cross and Red Crescent Societies (www. ifrc.org) is the world's largest humanitarian network, with nearly 100 million members, volunteers, and supporters in 186 National Societies.

means of inviting users worldwide to share our story while ensuring proper acknowledgement of the IFRC."

The IFRC uploaded these photos so they could be shared, which means people were free to copy, distribute, and transmit the photos with the following conditions:

- The photos must be attributed back to the IFRC,
- The photos could not be used for commercial purposes, and
- The photos must not be altered, transformed, or built upon.

"Creative Commons licenses allow us to open up our photos in good faith, trusting that these images will be used to both promote awareness of our work and dignify the people and places captured within them," Amy adds.

This type of Creative Commons licensing works well in situations where you want to get your imagery out there, but also want to protect the rights of your creative work. The flexibility of Creative Commons licensing allows you to tighten and loosen the rights based on your needs. Be sure to check out creativecommons.org to learn more.

 Submit Your Photos to Flickr Groups

With more than 4 billion photos,[3] Flickr is one of the largest photo-sharing sites and has what we think are some of the best social features. Flickr groups allow you to share content and conversation around a particular subject via a photo/video pool, discussion board, and maps. By submitting your photos to Flickr groups related to your cause, you are expanding your reach and awareness and opening yourself up to valuable networking opportunities.

What You Need   A Flickr account and some photos

How to Do It
1. Log in to Flickr and search for groups related to your cause at Flickr.com/groups.
2. Join the group and read the group rules.
3. Click on "Add Something," and submit relevant photos to the group pool and join the discussion.
4. Be sure to tag the photos too—adding tags helps categorize photos and makes them easier to find in a search.

A Closer Look   The best part about Flickr is that there is already a built-in community centered around photo sharing. Chances are that many of the members of this community care about your cause and actively participate in groups related to it. As with all social media, the key is to bring the content to them, and with Flickr groups, it is easy to do just that.

---

[3]Heather Champ, "$4,000,000,000," Flickr, October 12, 2009, http://blog.flickr.net/en/2009/10/12/4000000000.

The "Global warming—we CAN stop it!!! / Earth in DANGER. . ." (www.flickr.com/groups/globalwarmingwecanstopit/) Flickr group was started to increase awareness about global warming. When searching for Global Warming and Flickr, this group comes up first in Google organic search. With more than 1300 members, it is a fairly large group, featuring nearly 6000 items (photos, etc.) and an active discussion board. Nonprofits including Greenpeace USA and United Nations have posted to this group.

As visitors browse through the photos, they can link directly to each organization's complete photo stream. In fact, this social aspect of photo sharing is the very reason why we recommend doing it. By tagging your photos and submitting them to groups, you are greatly improving the chances that a potential supporter will find your content, and ultimately, support your cause.

CHAPTER 2

Communicate

Social media provide new and innovative ways to do what we've been doing for the ages—communicating. Communication should be a two-way street (if you do it right); otherwise, it's just marketing. This chapter will provide tactics for furthering your social media message, while the next will help you take your communications one step further to the engagement level. That's where the magic happens!

Just as the previous chapter provided tactics to help you set up accounts to be on brand, it is equally important to communicate on message and tone. While social media is by nature a bit more laid back, it is important to be consistent with your organization's overall voice. If there are multiple people contributing, this is even more important. When communicating as a team, be sure to use the free tools that are available to help coordinate. And, be sure you have a process and procedures manual for everyone on your team so everyone is on the same page.

When it comes to content, think of it as social capital. If what you are putting out there doesn't contribute to the community, keep it to yourself! Twitter is not a megaphone and Facebook isn't a bulletin board. You want to be sure that you are providing a regular stream of content that is relevant, interesting, and engaging to your supporters.

And, just because you post it on Twitter doesn't mean that everyone will see it. The key is to make your content travel. Make it easy to share with hashtags and Really Simple Syndication (RSS), and integrate it throughout all channels. Social media in and of itself is not a strategy. It is simply a vehicle to disseminate your broader message.

Finally, leverage the power of the platform. There are many unique features for each platform. Be sure to explore them and provide your supporters a rich experience.

18 Use Collaboration Tools to Manage Twitter Accounts

Even though Twitter is getting more rigid in its policies for third-party applications, more than 40 percent of tweets come from "non-official" apps. In fact, the farther away you get from Twitter's "official" apps, the more functionality you get. Third-party applications like CoTweet and Hootsuite help social media teams of two or more manage their workflow by supporting scheduled tweets, assigned tweets, multiple users, monitoring, and social network aggregation.

What You Need A Twitter account, a social media team of two or more, and a Twitter application that supports multiple users, like CoTweet or Hootsuite

How to Do It
1. Choose an application. The best part is, most of them provide a basic version for free, so try them out and see which one works best for your organization.
2. Build a process for scheduling and responding to tweets.
3. Provide access to administrators.
4. Meet regularly to refine process.

A Closer Look Like many people getting started in social media, when staffers at the National Building Museum first started setting up

The National Building Museum (www.nbm.org) advances the quality of the built environment by educating people about its impact on their lives.

accounts for the organization, they didn't really have a formal process or strategy in place. According to Brett Rodgers, the Museum's online marketing and communications manager, only later did they make sure it was something they were taking seriously and strategizing about. Now, the organization has a team of three people for whom social media is a part of their daily routine with tools in place to help them coordinate.

One of the Building Museum's most active channels is Twitter, and the team shares responsibility for managing the @buildingmuseum account. The team uses collaboration tools to schedule tweets, respond to tweets and messages, and monitor searches on key hashtags and programs. CoTweet helps the team coordinate and implement its strategy (see Exhibit 2.1). It also enables others to occasionally log in and schedule tweets on a program-to-program basis.

Brett says, "CoTweet and Hootsuite assist us in allowing multiple admins to manage Twitter accounts without tripping over each other. They currently work well and provide a better interface than Twitter's main web site in terms of taking in everything at once and are much better at keeping track of tweets, replies, mentions, and searches."

Exhibit 2.1   National Building Museum's CoTweet page

Source: © 2011 National Building Museum, www.nbm.org; CoTweet

Create Twitter Lists

Twitter lists provide nonprofits with a unique opportunity to organize other users into specific categories. Visitors to the organization's page can view and/or follow a list and read tweets from only users in that list. This provides a great way for a nonprofit to promote unique segments of its organization, including staff or chapters. The key is to create a relevant list that people will benefit from by having the ability to view tweets specific to the subject area.

What You Need   A Twitter account and the Twitter handles of everyone you want to put on the list

How to Do It
1. Visit the profile of the first member you'd like to add to the list, and click the list drop-down menu next to the message button.
2. Click "Create list" and name the list, provide an optional description, and click the "public" option.
3. For subsequent additions, simply select the existing list from the list drop-down menu.
4. It is important to note that lists require regular maintenance, so you may not want to create the allotted 20 lists that Twitter lets you make unless you want to spend the time to keep them all updated.

A Closer Look   Heifer International works all over the globe, and the organization touches many different areas—from sustainable agriculture and international development to fair trade and local food. "We created Twitter lists with the goal of better following Heifer's growing universe of Twitter connections," says Casey Neese, Heifer International's social media manager. "This way, we can find certain

Heifer International (www.heifer.org) is a global development nonprofit that works to end hunger and poverty by providing livestock and training to small-holder farmers in more than 50 countries.

Exhibit 2.2   Heifer International's Twitter list page
Source: Courtesy of Heifer International; Twitter

users when we want to engage them in an online conversation. These lists comprise a sort of Twitter Rolodex."

Heifer International's 20 Twitter lists include focus areas such as development, local food, and sustainability (see Exhibit 2.2). The organization uses the lists feature to connect with niche groups of supporters. It also uses Twitter lists for internal teams, so they can easily follow media, bloggers, staff, and volunteers.

Two of the organization's most popular lists are the sustainability and philanthropy lists. "So far, our lists are being discovered organically," says Casey. "I think we're now at the point where we can start to direct traffic to some of our lists in the hopes of drawing more users into the conversations we're having."

Display Names of Staff Contributing to Twitter and Facebook

Building real relationships is one of the key benefits of using social media, and adding a personal touch to these channels can help your community see the people behind the brand. Many nonprofits use the background of their Twitter page to display photos of staff members who contribute to their feed, or use annotations in direct messages. On Facebook, page administrators can be displayed via a badge. Use personalization like this if you're looking for high levels of engagement and two-way communication, or just want to give credit where credit is due!

What You Need   A Twitter account, a Facebook page, artwork and photos, and a graphic designer for layout

How to Do It   To display staff members in the background of your organization's Twitter page:

1. Collect names, job titles, photos, and Twitter handles from the staff members who contribute to your Twitter account.
2. Decide what information you want to display to the public. It's common to simply use photos, names, and sometimes Twitter handles (e.g., Chad Norman, @chadnorman).
3. Create a custom Twitter background graphic using an image editor.
4. Integrate the team photos, names, and other information into the design of your background. If you're not a designer, find one, or use an online tool like mytweetspace.com or twitbacks.com to help you build a background.
5. Access the "Settings" of your organization's Twitter account.
6. Press the "Change background image" button on the Design tab.
7. Upload your image, and visit your profile to see how it looks.

To display staff members on your organization's Facebook page:

1. Press the "Edit Page" button on your organization's page.
2. Click the "Featured" link in the left hand column.
3. Press the "Add Featured Page Owners" button.
4. Select the administrators you want to display, and press OK.
5. Visit your page to see how it looks.

A Closer Look   If you're doing it right, communicating via social media should feel like a personal, one-on-one conversation. The

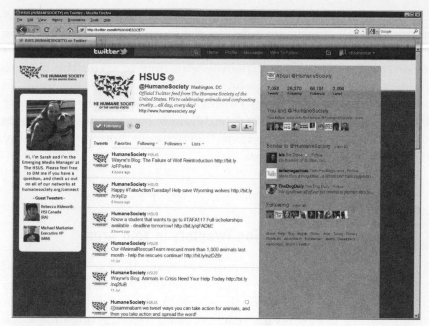

Exhibit 2.3   Humane Society of the United States Twitter page

Source: Courtesy of The Humane Society of The United States; Twitter

Humane Society of the United States (HSUS) maintains a high-level of interaction with its supporters on Twitter by replying, retweeting, and reaching out on a regular basis, so putting a name and face behind all this activity can help.

To make these communications seem more authentic and human, HSUS has disclosed who is tweeting on behalf of the organization via a custom Twitter background graphic (see Exhibit 2.3). Carie Lewis, HSUS's director of emerging media, sums this up well: "On our Twitter background, you see our faces with our pets and immediately have an idea of who we are and why you'd want to talk to us—we're animal lovers."

The organization's Twitter background graphic contains some great branding elements (see Tactic 5), but also features the three staff members who are tweeting on the account. The name, title, photo, and description are displayed for the emerging media manager, who is the primary staff member behind the account. It also shows the name and photos of the back tweeters, along with a set of initials which can be used for identification in tweets and direct messages.

Over time, this tactic has helped HSUS be a more authentic, responsive, and effective member of the social community by putting a human face on its Twitter activity. Carie adds, "People don't trust a logo, they trust real people who they've taken the time to connect with. Many times people obtain misinformation about us on the Internet, and turn to Twitter to talk about it. Because we're listening, we can have an open and honest conversation with them to clear things up, and in turn they trust us and become more engaged in what we're doing."

 21   **Connect with the Top Tweeters in Your Area**

Reaching out to the Twitter community is an effective way to spread your message beyond your typical group of supporters. Whether you are launching a key campaign, advocating a particular issue, or simply wanting to expand the reach of your blog, targeting individuals and building relationships can bring real results. There are tools that can help you identify the most followed and active tweeters in your local area, but you also want to look for key influencers based on their clout. Build a list, then build some relationships, and you'll be ready to go when your next social media campaign needs an extra push.

What You Need   A Twitter account and a local area to serve

How to Do It
1. Visit www.twitaholic.com and search for your own Twitter handle.
2. Find this line of text: "Ranked XX in their location on twitaholic! (by followers in 'YourCity, YourState')."
3. Click the link for your city and state.
4. Collect the user names for the top tweeters on this list.
5. Repeat for other cities by manipulating the URL in your browser's location field.

A Closer Look   If your organization has a mission that focuses on a geographic area, it is wise to get to know the local social media

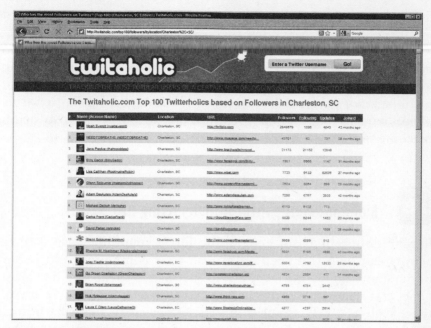

Exhibit 2.4   Twitaholic's search results page for Charleston, SC
Source: Courtesy of the Twitaholic

influencers (see Exhibit 2.4). This group of key people can help extend the reach of your message into the local community, which is why building relationships with them is critical. Once you identify who these key influencers are, you can begin building a rapport that will bring mutual benefit to you both.

There are a few actions you can take that can help build a more natural relationship with these key influencers. These actions are all very subtle, but when used together they can effectively turn these influencers into supporters who can help your cause.

Using your organization's Twitter account, you can:

- Follow the Twitter accounts of key influencers.
- Reach out to key influencers by name.
- Retweet key influencers if they share relevant content.
- Reply to key influencers with an answer if they ask a mission-related question.
- Direct message key influencers with questions and comments.
- If they are helping, give these key influencers a "Follow Friday."

Once you do these things and begin to build a relationship, it will be much easier to request their help in the future. For instance, you may want to ask them to tweet or retweet a timely message. You may need to direct message them for information or ask them to help with an issue. And eventually you may want to ask them to blog about a campaign or program (see Tactic 57). Having a local Twitter army of influencers ready when you need it can be helpful, so begin reaching out as soon as you can.

 ## Monitor Local Twitter Activity Using Hashtags

If your nonprofit has a geographic focus, following local Twitter activity can help you keep an eye on your community and better understand how your supporters are using social media. Most cities and states have active hashtags that can be monitored in real time, such as #NYC, #SFO, and #FL. Other cities, like Charleston, SC, have sets of local hashtags for different topics, such as #chsbiz (business) and #chsgreen (sustainability). Watching these conversations in an RSS reader or Twitter client can help your organization better understand how your community feels about issues and will teach you what you need to know in order to join the conversation.

What You Need   Local Twitter hashtags and an RSS reader or Twitter client

How to Do It
1. Determine what geographic area you want to monitor, such as your neighborhood, city, state, region, or country.
2. Use hashtag directory sites like hashtags.org to see which conversations are active and worth monitoring.
3. Go to http://search.twitter.com and search for the hashtags you want to monitor.
4. Collect the RSS feed for each hashtag you want to follow. On the search results page, look for the "Feed for This Query" link in the upper right.
5. Monitor each of these feeds in an RSS reader, such as Google Reader. You can also view these feeds via a Twitter client, such as TweetDeck or Seesmic, or by plugging them into RSS widgets, such as iGoogle.

A Closer Look Listening and responding via hashtags is an easy and effective way to get involved with your local Twitter community. Whether you are monitoring hashtag activity using Twitter.com, columns on TweetDeck, or a listening dashboard, this treasure trove of real-time information can easily be acted upon to help drive your mission.

You should start by looking for local hashtags that have a lot of activity. Sometimes hashtags will be the initials of a city (e.g., #nyc or #la), but often they will be the full name (e.g., #miami or #dallas). If your organization has a wider appeal, you can monitor the hashtags for entire states (e.g., #CA or #GA). Also, be sure to check out the hashtag for you local airport's abbreviation, because in some cases it has become the de facto channel for local content (e.g., #chs).

Once you've identified the hashtags you want to follow, you'll want to start listening. It's very easy to use search.twitter. com to look at hashtag activity, but it can be time-consuming and cumbersome (see Exhibit 2.5). If you're using a Twitter client like TweetDeck or Seesmic, you can easily monitor activity throughout the day by adding columns for specific hashtags. It can also be

Exhibit 2.5 Twitter search results page for the #nyc hashtag
Source: Courtesy of Twitter

helpful to set up a shared dashboard created in iGoogle, or use a service like Radian6, to allow for listening across your entire organization.

Once you have your monitoring tools set up, it's time to think about how you will act upon the information you see. It's smart to set up a response plan for your organization that lays out how you should react to each piece of relevant content, as this will help reduce decision-making time and help you respond in a timely manner. Some of the actions you can take as a result of this activity include:

- Promoting key messages to a local audience by attaching the appropriate hashtag.
- Listening and responding to your local area by monitoring specific hashtags.
- Retweeting important local messages that appeal to the entire community.
- Understanding how your local audience uses Twitter in general.
- Adding your voice to local conversations, even if they are off-mission—get involved!

With all the local chatter out there, your organization needs to be listening in order to be an effective member of the community. Once you get into the habit of listening, you'll wonder how you ever got by without it!

 ## Make Your Tweets Retweetable

When Twitter users retweet (RT) your tweet, they are giving it a vote of confidence to their own network that it is interesting and worth reading. There are two types of RTs, *official* or *native* Twitter RTs that show the original author of the tweet and can't be edited; and traditional RTs (still embraced by most of the Twitter community) that allow you to add commentary and "own" the tweet. For the sake of the latter style, keep your tweets retweetable!

What You Need   A Twitter account and a little math

How to Do It

1. The key to making your tweets retweetable is to make them short enough that users opting for the traditional RT method can RT them without editing and possibly even add some of their own commentary.

2. Find your magic number! Start by counting the characters in your Twitter handle. Add one for a space, one for the @ symbol, and two for RT. (i.e.,: for @nonprofit: you would start with nine for the handle, add two for spaces, one for "@", one for ":", and two for RT = 15).

3. Leave at least that many characters remaining in your tweet. (More, if you can, to encourage commenting.)

A Closer Look Most "unofficial" applications give users the option of RTing in the traditional style or the new style, but the interface varies. Let's take a look at the official and unofficial ways to RT:

Twitter (web)

• Hover over a tweet.
• Click the retweet link for an official RT.
• The tweet will then be forwarded to all of your followers.
• For the traditional style RT, copy and paste the tweet, adding "RT @username" to the beginning.

Twitter (mobile)

• Select the tweet.
• For the official RT, click the RT icon.
• For the traditional RT, it's a bit harder. Click the forward icon and then "Quote Tweet." You can then add your own commentary.

TweetDeck

• TweetDeck has a lot of fans because of this simple feature. Users can choose to RT in the official (Retweet now) or the traditional style (Edit then retweet) simply by selecting the method in the settings. Since it was acquired by Twitter in 2011, it will be interesting to monitor how the application evolves.

HootSuite

• HootSuite also has a hybrid approach to the RT. They provide what they call an "on-the-fly" choice of styles for each individual message. Users click the retweet option at the top right of a tweet and then have the option of what style they would like to use.

 ## Sign up for Tweets for Good

When Twitter launched its Promoted Tweets platform in 2010, it launched with six businesses and two nonprofits. Since that time, Twitter has donated Promoted Tweets to many nonprofit organizations through its Promoted Tweets for Good program. Promoted Tweets are the regular tweets from a user account that organizations want to highlight to a wider group of users. The tweets surface in Twitter's search results and in users' timelines, and then the users actually become part of the process. If the Promoted Tweet doesn't receive much interaction, it will disappear from the ad platform, creating a unique ad experience where engaging messages are rewarded.

What You Need   A Twitter account and a promotion-worthy campaign that is scheduled to occur at least four months in the future

How to Do It
   1. Sign-up at hope140.org.

A Closer Look   Claire Diaz Ortiz, who runs social innovation and philanthropy at Twitter, advises nonprofits to apply early to promote their future campaigns. "Our pro-bono promoted Tweets for Good program offers select nonprofit organizations the chance to run pro-bono Promoted Tweets for a term of up to one month at a time on Twitter," she says. "Organizations should apply with a specific campaign or two in mind and with ideal campaign dates at least four months in the future."

   Tweets for Good is just one of Twitter's philanthropic outreach efforts that is part of its hope140 program at hope140.org (see Exhibit 2.6). Twitter has aligned itself with many key nonprofits including American Red Cross, Room to Read, Global Citizen Year, and charity: water. The company has also stepped up its promotional

Exhibit 2.6   Hope140.org home page
Source: Courtesy of Twitter

efforts around recent disasters including earthquake relief in Japan (#hope4japan) and in support of Hope for Haiti Now.

The recently launched #betternow project on the hope140 .org site serves as a resource center for nonprofits that features case studies of how leading nonprofits are uniquely using Twitter to advance their missions.

Nonprofits that want to run a longer campaign and have more control over timing can opt to invest in the regular Promoted Tweets service. According to Tammy Gordon, AARP's director of social communications, the membership organization serving people 50 and older targeted Twitter users talking about Social Security or NASCAR. Its Promoted Tweets campaign also played into breaking news. When Elizabeth Taylor passed away, the team tweeted a bunch of links to her career. "We were frustrated by the lack of targeting beyond keywords, obviously we'd like to also target by age, but we did see a dramatic increase in followers," Tammy says. "Within two months, our Twitter followers doubled."

Recruit New Staff and Volunteers

Whether you are looking to fill a position at your organization, or are in need of some last-minute volunteers, where better than your organization's social networks to turn for your recruiting efforts? Members of these networks are opted in, and therefore, already engaged with your cause. And, with the real-time nature of social media, you can get your message out quickly, which comes in very handy for last-minute projects or disaster response efforts.

What You Need   Presence on social networking sites, followers, and job listings or volunteer opportunities

How to Do it
1. Take an audit of your social networking presence. Twitter, Facebook, and LinkedIn should top the list for this tactic (depending on your target audience).
2. Determine if there are any other platforms where you can extend your outreach—that is, consider adding a volunteer incentive to your organization's Foursquare specials or adding Craigslist to your arsenal.
3. Determine the best time and day to reach your audience. If you are trying to reach moms with kids, during the day may be the best time, whereas if you are trying to reach professionals, a Saturday morning may be your best bet.
4. Craft your message. Ideally, your social network outreach should lead to more information on your site.

A Closer Look   What started as one mother's gift in 2001 has grown into a massive volunteer operation. In an effort to be as efficient as possible, Baby Buggy relies heavily on its volunteer force of 5,000 people to help twice a day with bundling, patching, and sorting donated items.

> Baby Buggy (www.babybuggy.org) is dedicated to providing families in need across the United States with essential equipment, clothing, and products for their infants and young children.

Baby Buggy has relied on social media to help grow its pool of volunteers and donations, increasing access, visibility, and awareness for the organization and its needs.

"Our foray into social media happened in 2008," says Katherine Snider, Baby Buggy's executive director. "We thought 'there has to be a better way to communicate than to meet and pile information on people.' I was really resistant because I didn't understand it from a personal point of view, but I can't tell you how quickly our following has grown and how effective it has been."

When Baby Buggy encounters a real-time need, like a coat shortage during winter, staff can tweet out a call for donations and volunteers and receive an immediate response. Katherine credits much of the organization's success in reaching volunteers online to the fact that moms, Baby Buggy's primary constituency, are among early adopters of social media.

 ## Start, Join, and Organize Conversations with Hashtags

One of the most practical applications of using hashtags is to organize conversations. By placing the "#" symbol before a keyword in a tweet, the message is categorized and a live link is automatically generated that leads to a search on other tweets containing that hashtag. This is useful for monitoring a topic, creating a filtered view of your Twitter stream, or pulling specific conversations into other platforms, such as web pages or live feeds displayed at an event (see Tactic 29).

What You Need   A Twitter account and a unique hashtag

How to Do It
1. To start a conversation around a specific hashtag, determine the hashtag you want to use.
2. Make the hashtag relevant and meaningful, but as short and unique as possible.
3. Head over to Hashtags.org and search for the hashtag to make sure it isn't already being used.

4. To join a conversation, simply include the existing hashtag in your tweets.

5. To organize or monitor a conversation, click on the hashtag and the live results will be displayed.

A Closer Look   Chances are that if you're reading this book, you're interested in nonprofit technology. Well, a simple little hashtag has made it easy to follow along with the broader nonprofit technology conversation happening all over the Web.

NPTECH was created as a tag for use in social networking sites like Delicious and Flickr so nonprofit technology professionals could share and refer information. According to nonprofit technology guru Peter Campbell, NPTECH also refers to "the broad, loose community of socially minded professionals who work with technology, be it servers or social media, at mission-minded organizations."

The term has evolved as social sites have and #nptech is now the hashtag to follow on Twitter for the latest nonprofit technology news, conversation, and resources. People simply add the hashtag to relevant tweets, making it easier to follow all tweets related to the topic (see Exhibit 2.7).

Exhibit 2.7   Twitter search results page for the #nptech hashtag
Source: Courtesy of Twitter

Whether it is nonprofit technology you're interested in or the #oilspill, hashtags make it easy to centralize topical content and discussion. If you log in to Twitter, you can see the trending topics, or you can create one of your own around a topic your organization is interested in.

 ## Promote an Event or Campaign with a Hashtag

Although some hashtags (see Tactic 24) surface organically within the Twitter community, there are many that are part of a well-devised marketing plan. A great way to use hashtags is to promote an event or campaign with them. You may choose to do pre-promotion for your event by using a hashtag or just spread the word about the official hashtag at the event so people can follow along with the back-channel conversation.

What You Need   An event or campaign, a Twitter account, and a unique hashtag

How to Do It
1. Prior to the launch of marketing for an event or campaign, determine a hashtag to use to organize conversation on Twitter (see Tactic 24).
2. Once a hashtag is determined, be sure to promote it in all of your marketing materials and start using it whenever you tweet about the subject.
3. Be sure all stakeholders know to use the hashtag too.
4. While onsite, take every chance you get to promote use of the hashtag.
5. Display the hashtag feed throughout the event and virtually on your web site.

A Closer Look   Each year, the nonprofit tech (#nptech) community gathers to learn all about the latest advancements in technology at The Nonprofit Technology Network's (NTEN) Nonprofit Technology Conference (NTC). Before and during the 2011 event, attendees networked and shared resources and social event information by using the hashtag #11NTC.

NTEN (www.nten.org) aspires to a world where all nonprofit organizations skillfully and confidently use technology to meet community needs and fulfill their missions.

According to Holly Ross, NTEN's executive director, the organization had three goals for using the hashtag:

1. Create one real-time stream of information to make navigating the show much easier,
2. Use the hashtag to build a sense of community amongst the folks using it, and
3. Use individual session hashtags as a form of note-taking at the event.

NTEN has built the hashtag into the branding of the conference, referring to the show as #11NTC, including it in e-mails, session introductions, and even on name badge cards. During the 2011 conference, the #11NTC hashtag was used more than 12,000 times, becoming a trending topic on Twitter.

"It's an interesting way to also excite folks who didn't know about the event and get them queued up to attend in the next year!" says Holly.

28 Contribute to Mission-Related Twitter Hashtags

Hashtags help organize social chatter on Twitter, and nonprofits can use them to integrate messages and content into mission-related conversations. During disasters, political debates, and key events, some hashtags become real-time feeds of social conversations. Other hashtags are associated with places, ideas, and things people love, and these conversations are active throughout the year. Joining these conversations can help contribute to the community, reach a new audience, and drive traffic to your web site.

What You Need A Twitter account, content to share, and a web analytics tool

How to Do It

1. Learn what hashtags are and how to find some that relate to
   your mission (see Tactic 20).
2. Create a plan for when and what you will add to the conversation. Blog content, videos, retweets of important messages,
   and original statements are all good choices.
3. Add hashtags to your tweets (#NYC, #climatechange, #high-
   ered) when you post updates.
4. Monitor the hashtags to continue the conversation. If someone retweets you, thank them. If someone responds to one of
   your tweets, keep the conversation going.
5. Use analytics tools to measure the reach and impact of these
   tweets. You can measure the reach of your messages using
   TweetReach (see Tactic 97), any increase in Twitter followers,
   and referrals from Twitter.com using a web analytics tool.

A Closer Look Jumping in to any conversation can be intimidating,
which is why first getting to know the participants is a great place
to start. Nonprofits can learn a lot by listening to the chatter on
Twitter hashtags, and this is great way to determine where your
organization's voice may fit in best. Once a few hashtags are identified,
there are many different ways to join the conversation.

When current events and Twitter are used together, hashtags
become a conduit for information. During disasters, nonprofits
can add resources and support to the conversation (e.g., #haiti,
#japan, #oilspill, #flooding). Organizations like The American Red
Cross, The National Wildlife Federation, NCRC, and The Ocean
Conservancy all contributed to one of these hashtags.

Twitter hashtags often become active during current affairs,
like key legislation debates or pressing human rights issues, and are
used to organize and share information. In 2009, groups like The
Environmental Defense Fund rallied around the #aces hashtag
during the debate over the American Clean Energy and Security
Act. The #climatechange hashtag is used year round, and nonprofits
like WWF Australia and The Windfall Center have added it to their
tweets and joined the worldwide discussion (see Exhibit 2.8).

Other hashtags collect tweets that are for groups of nonprofits,
such as #highered, #animalrights, #foundation, and #arts. The Florida
State University College of Education tweeted about an article discussing the issue of testing teachers, and the #highered hashtag

Exhibit 2.8   Twitter search results page for the #climatechange hashtag
Source: Courtesy of Twitter

was attached helping it reach a larger audience. These nonprofit industry hashtags are a great place to expose your Twitter channel to a new crowd and contribute something meaningful to the community.

 ## Use TwitPic to Share Photos and Videos

TwitPic lets users share photos and videos on Twitter in real time. With more than 60 million unique people visiting the site per month and 25 million users, TwitPic has quickly risen to become one of the 100 top-trafficked web sites. It provides nonprofits with a very valuable platform for sharing their work through images and video. It also provides nonprofits some special perks that you have to be "in the know" to get (read on).

What You Need   A Twitter account, a web browser or mobile application, and a photo or video

How to Do It

1. Go to twitpic.com and log in with your Twitter account information (this will enable you to post to Twitter directly from TwitPic).
2. Click on "Upload Photo or Video" from the top navigation.
3. Browse to attach the file.
4. Add a description, which will ultimately be your tweet. (Think of this as your caption.)
5. Alternately, most apps have direct integration with TwitPic, you just have to select it as the default media service in the settings.

A Closer Look   Like many other social platforms, TwitPic has worked with a handful of nonprofits to get them up and running on its service by providing one-on-one support and training. However, there currently isn't a formalized nonprofit program. According to TwitPic founder Noah Everett, the company is looking into providing free advertising for special nonprofit campaigns or events, so be sure to keep checking in!

Here are a couple of ways that social good organizations are using TwitPic:

- Working with TwitPic, UNICEF (twitpic.com/photos/UNICEF) had the standard character limit removed for captions and uses TwitPic as a storytelling platform through photo captions. Each photo tells a mini-story of the organization's work and who it is helping.
- Tom's Shoes uses TwitPic (twitpic.com/photos/tomsshoes) to share photos with its Twitter followers. The company shares photos of shoes being donated, staff photos, fan photos, and behinds the scenes shots of their operations.

30   Display RSS Feeds on Your Web Site

RSS stands for *Really Simple Syndication*, and provides a regularly updated feed of links and information, whether it be news headlines, photos, or blog entries. Among the many benefits to adding an RSS widget on your web site include providing fresh content to the site and increasing your organization's search engine optimization (SEO). It is very simple to do and will provide your web site visitors with automatically published dynamic content without your web developer having to work overtime.

What You Need   A plan for what content you'd like to aggregate, an RSS widget application (for this example, we will use RSSinclude), and a web developer.

How to Do It
1. Visit rssinclude.com.
2. Click on the "Create New RSSbox" link.
3. Choose the template you'd like to use for your news feed.
4. Enter the RSS feed that you want to pull in. (Or, subscribe to a premium box to pull in more than one feed.)
5. Style the box.
6. Create a login for RSSinclude.com.
7. Copy and paste the HTML/Javascript or PHP code into your site.

A Closer Look   Nonprofit technologist Peter Campbell has long hailed the benefits of RSS, not only for nonprofit web sites, but also as a consumption tool for nonprofit professionals.

"The best reason to incorporate RSS feeds into a web site is to provide for currency—fresh news and information that is automatically updated," says Peter. "While this doesn't do away with the need for original content, it supplements it, which can be useful if your original content output is limited, as it keeps the web site fresh for visitors."

When it comes to selecting RSS sources, Peter advises to choose carefully, not only examining the quality of articles, but also the pertinence to your cause, and continuously monitoring what is being pulled in. According to Peter, a good place to start is to look at the web sites your staff is already monitoring for information relating to your mission. He also suggests considering looking at internal information that could be aggregated into a feed, such as job and event listings.

Finally, Peter recommends putting RSS to work for you. "RSS flips the Web surfing paradigm—it brings the Web to you," he says. Instead of visiting your five go-to web sites each morning, with RSS, you can streamline the process by subscribing to feeds from the sites and consuming the content in one central location.

"If you're using a full-featured RSS reader, like Google Reader, you can easily share, save, or publish (in RSS format) the articles that are important to you," says Peter. "In fact, this becomes a way to create a curated list of articles that you can subsequently publish to your web site."

 Display Live Twitter Content on Your Web Site and Blog

Integrating the social experience into your organization's web site will help promote the channel, engage supporters, and provide a constant source of dynamic content. Twitter widgets make it easy to embed real-time tweets from your organization's account, a particular hashtag, or a list of Twitter users (e.g., staff, volunteers, or board members). When placed on a web site or blog, the latest updates will be displayed providing your visitors with fresh, current, useful content related to your mission. This visibility will also increase awareness of your Twitter activity, which will attract new followers and expand the reach of the channel.

What You Need   A Twitter account and access to your web site and blog files

How to Do It   Determine what you want to display on your web site or blog. Examples include: Your organization's Twitter feed, a hashtag from an event you're hosting, a hashtag of a movement you are participating in, or the feed from a Twitter list.

1. Visit www.twitter.com/about/resources/widgets.
2. Click "My Website" in the left navigation.
3. Select the type of widget you want to use.
4. Enter all the settings, customize the look and feel, then press the "Finish & Grab Code" button.
5. Insert the provided code into the appropriate files on your web site and blog.
6. Test the widget to ensure it is working and looks good.

A Closer Look Having meaningful conversations and activity on Twitter can create real impact, but you'll also want to use that chatter to reach a new audience. Bringing the conversation onto your web site or blog shines a spotlight on this social activity and encourages other supporters to join in.

The most common way to integrate Twitter into a web site is to embed the profile widget, which will provide real-time updates from your organization. Nonprofits such as The Sierra Club and Greenpeace USA display Twitter feeds featuring updates from their own accounts, giving Web visitors a live glimpse into their social streams. This helps to spread their message and also provides an easy source of dynamic content.

Live tweets can also be pulled in using the Twitter application programming interface (API) to create rich experiences for supporters. The National Wildlife Federation (NWF) displays tweets featuring the #NWF hashtag on its Wildlife Watch web site (see Exhibit 2.9). NWF encourages nature lovers everywhere to tweet about wildlife and include the hashtag #NWF. On its web site, NWF

Exhibit 2.9   National Wildlife Federation's Wildlife Watch Twitter page
Source: Courtesy of the National Wildlife Federation

imports and displays these updates in real time, giving wildlife watchers a live glimpse of nature sightings around the country.

Capitalizing on an active Twitter stream is important for non-profits that are trying to increase communication through social activity. Using tactics like this will help you package and promote social conversations and create a successful program.

 Feed Your Blog to Twitter and Facebook

Posting blog content to Facebook and Twitter is an effective way to get it in front of supporters and prospects. However, depending on how your organization is staffed, remembering to do repetitive tasks like this can easily be overlooked. When your resources are limited, it might make sense to use a tool that can remember to publish your blog content to Twitter and Facebook so you don't have to. Socializing your blog content is needed to increase readership, so it never hurts to have a little help from technology.

What You Need   A blog with an RSS feed, a Facebook page, a Twitter account, and an account at Twitterfeed.com

How to Do It
1. Identify the RSS feed of a blog or other content stream you want to share on your organization's Twitter and Facebook accounts.
2. Create an account with twitterfeed.com, and follow the instructions to configure your settings.
3. Publish new blog content, and confirm that it is appearing on Twitter and Facebook in an acceptable fashion.

A Closer Look   For small organizations with limited staff and time, having blog content appear on Twitter and Facebook without any additional effort is helpful and as easy as it sounds. Once set up, posts typically appear on Twitter and Facebook with the blog post's title and short URL, but this can be configured to suit your needs.

With twitterfeed, you can customize how and when your posts appear on Twitter and Facebook. This provides the flexibility to manage how the title, description, and image are displayed when the update appears. The "Post Prefix" and "Post Suffix" fields allow for small statements to be added to automatic posts, which is handy when you want to start each update with "New from our blog:" as a setup for the post. You can also use keyword filtering to keep certain subjects from being posted.

Some of these features are there to hide the fact that the content is being automatically posted. Twitter and Facebook are living platforms, so content that is auto-posted can sometimes seem less human because of the stiff language. If you choose to post content automatically, configure the system to deliver the most human sounding updates possible, and you'll see better results.

 Use Facebook Social Plug-ins on Your Site

Even if you have the fastest coder in the world, nothing is going to beat the benefits of real-time updates of integrated content on your web site. One line of code can turn a static page into a page with dynamic content. Facebook's social plug-ins let visitors to your site see what their friends have liked, commented on or shared. Everyone has seen the Like button (see Tactic 12), however, there are seven more plugins that are worth exploring too.

What You Need   A Facebook account, a web site, and a web developer

How to Do It
1. Visit http://developers.facebook.com/docs/plugins/, and determine which plugin you'd like to use.
2. Once you select the plugin, scroll down to get the code.
3. Get the Open Graph Tabs.
4. Add the code to your site and test.

A Closer Look   As with all of Epic Change's campaigns (Tweetsgiving being the most notable), social media fuels the giving. For the "To Mama With Love" campaign that takes place around Mother's Day, the gurus at Epic Change built a highly-interactive web page that pulled in all of the social media activity into one central place by using video, a Twitter box, and a Facebook activity plugin (see Exhibit 2.10).

Exhibit 2.10   To Mama With Love home page
Source: Courtesy of To Mama With Love

Participants made a donation and created a "heartspace" in honor of their mother or loved one. The heartspace was then added to the interactive map. Visitors to the site could then "like" or share the heartspace. With the Facebook plugin, the likes and activity around the heartspaces was aggregated and displayed on the homepage.

"We really wanted to be able to spread the love from the site as far and wide as possible," says Stacey Monk, co-founder of Epic Change. "Highlighting beautiful, heartful content inspires more beautiful, heartful content—it sparks a movement. The plugin was an easy way for us to track and highlight content being shared from our site that was especially inspirational and impactful."

To Mama With Love (www.tomamawithlove.org) is a collaborative online art project created by Epic Change (epicchange.org) to honor "mamas" around the globe and to raise money to help women change the world. (More than $30,000 was raised in 2011.)

Add Events to Your Facebook Page

One of the most powerful features of your Facebook page is the ability to promote both private and public events. The benefits of creating a public event is that when people RSVP, it shows up in their activity feed, so their friends can, in turn, join in the fun. The event page features its own wall, so attendees can pre-network and organizers can drum up excitement. Page admins can also update fans and segment them demographically. Attendees can even check in at the event, extending the experience to the actual event.

What You Need   A Facebook page, an event to promote, and artwork

How to Do It
1. On the left hand side of your organization's Facebook page, click on "Events."
2. From there, you can choose to "Create an Event."
3. Complete the form by selecting the date and time, and adding the name of the event, the location, and information about the event.
4. Add [ticketed], [free], or [registration required] to event titles so attendees know if they need to buy tickets or register.
5. You also have the option of inviting your personal friends. If you would like to invite people who are not on Facebook, or that you're not friends with on Facebook, you can enter their e-mail addresses into the box on the "Guest List" tab of the Edit Event page.
6. Once submitted, click the "Update Fans Of" box in the upper right-hand corner.

A Closer Look   Charleston Waterkeeper used Facebook Events functionality to market its signature event, the Water Ball, held in

Charleston Waterkeeper (www.charlestonwaterkeeper.org) is dedicated to protecting the public's right to clean water by defending Charleston's waterways from pollution.

Exhibit 2.11   Charleston Waterkeeper's Facebook page
Source: © Charleston Waterkeeper; Facebook

April 2011. With an active Facebook community of nearly 3000 supporters, the organization started marketing the event in February (see Exhibit 2.11).

The organization allowed supporters to comment on the event wall, which was very active leading up to the event. Staff also posted updates leading up to the event to build excitement and sell tickets. The artwork for the iconic poster was revealed, photos from last year's event were posted, news appearances were publicized, and questions about dress code were answered. The key here was that it was engaging. One hundred seventy-two people RSVPed for the event on Facebook. The event itself drew more than 350 people and grossed $31,000 for the organization.

"Facebook provides an incredibly valuable platform for non-profits and businesses alike to capture and consolidate the attention of thousands of potential supporters," says Cyrus Buffum, founder of Charleston Waterkeeper. "These eyeballs may already be fixed on your cause; it's then just a matter of encouraging them to take the next step—participation."

Here are some tips for making the most out of your event page:

- Encourage people to share the event link via the "Share" link at the top of the page.
- Encourage attendees to invite their friends by pressing the "Select Guests to Invite" button under the event artwork.
- Use the wall to build up buzz before the event and to provide pertinent event reminders leading up to the event.
- Use the wall to provide a recap and to thank attendees for coming to the event.
- Post pictures and video of the event.
- Provide a "save the date" for next year's event.

 Integrate Other Social Channels with Facebook

For many nonprofits, Facebook is the biggest and most active channel in their social program. This makes Facebook a wonderful place to integrate content from other social channels, like Twitter or YouTube. Custom tabs and applications, like those developed by Involver, make it very easy to bring tweets, photos, and videos directly into Facebook. Having a tab featuring YouTube videos or live Twitter updates increases the value of your page and promotes these channels to your Facebook community. Make Facebook your non-profit's one-stop social media shop!

What You Need   A Facebook account, other social accounts (e.g., Twitter, YouTube, or Flickr), and a Facebook application like Involver

How to Do It
1. Identify which social channels you want to display on your organization's Facebook page.
2. Visit www.involver.com/applications and press "Install" button associated with the platform you want to use (e.g., Twitter).
3. Select the page where you want to install the application.
4. Allow Facebook and the application to communicate, and provide Involver with your name and phone number.
5. Enter the Twitter account name or search criteria you wish to display via the application. You can also set the maximum number of tweets to display.

6. Press the "Save Changes" button, then return to your organization's Facebook page to confirm the installation (this may take a few minutes).

A Closer Look   Thanks to Facebook's use of applications, creating custom content for your organization's page is fairly straight forward. Content from Twitter, YouTube, and Flickr can be displayed on custom tabs (see Tactic 35) by simply embedding widgets and players from each service. For a more customized, integrated experience, many nonprofits turn to Facebook application companies like Involver.

Involver offers free use of up to two of its basic apps, which include Twitter, YouTube, and Flickr. These apps are easy to install, offer a clean user experience, and look great on Facebook pages. For instance, the Twitter application will put your organization's feed on its own tab, include a "Follow" button, and place a nice icon in the left navigation. This takes about three minutes to set up, and is the easiest way to get Twitter content onto your Facebook page. The YouTube app is just as easy to set up, and allows you to set a featured video and include a detailed playlist.

There are many great examples of nonprofits using Involver to integrate social channels into their Facebook presence. The Ronald McDonald House Charities has custom tabs featuring Twitter updates and YouTube videos that are powered by Involver apps. The Art Institute of Chicago uses Involver to deliver tweets and Flickr photos, and YouTube Video Box to bring in its YouTube content.

Some nonprofits are integrating emerging social networks into their Facebook page, such as The Art Institute of Chicago's social gaming tab featuring SCVNGR. The Smithsonian brings a live experience to its Facebook fans by integrating a Ustream.tv channel into its page. Streaming live video is a powerful way to communicate with supporters (see Tactic 41), and Facebook's news feed provides the perfect channel for attracting live viewers. So regardless of where your social program takes you, remember that Facebook is a great place to bring it all together and give your supporters access to everything.

 Include Social Channels in Contact Information

As a valuable channel in your marketing communications strategy, social media links should be included alongside other contact information for your organization. Including your Facebook page, Twitter account, and blog will help promote those channels, but also look at including other platforms like YouTube, Flickr, and foursquare. Remember that different supporters will want to reach you in different ways, so include these social channels in addition to traditional contact methods on your web site, business cards, advertisements, and fliers. If being there for your supporters is important, give them the opportunity to reach out in any way possible.

What You Need   Social media accounts, a graphic designer, and access to your organization's web site

How to Do It

1. Determine which social media channels should be included. It is most common to see Facebook and Twitter, but if you're using other channels, you should include them as well.
2. Decide how you want to display this information. Some organizations like to use those nice juicy social media icons, while others take a natural language approach and use hyperlinks (e.g., "Follow us on Twitter").
3. Update your web site to include these new channels. Definitely put them on your contact page, and consider including links in the header or footer of your web site's template.
4. Update your organization's business card template. This is an important one, and will take a little more thought. You may want your organization's Facebook and Twitter links on each card, but also consider allowing individuals to include their own Twitter or blog when appropriate.
5. Make sure your designers know to include these links on print materials when appropriate. Use text links if possible, like facebook.com/YourOrg.

A Closer Look   If you're managing a social media program for a nonprofit, you know how often supporters use these channels as a point of contact with the organization. While it's common to be fielding direct messages from Twitter, questions on Facebook wall posts, and inquiries buried in YouTube comments, nonprofits rarely include these social channels on web site contact pages.

Many nonprofit web sites prominently feature social channels throughout the template, ensuring they are visible on each page.

Organizations like The United Way, The Boys and Girls Clubs of America, CARE, and World Wildlife Fund all do this well, and in these cases, social links are clearly visible on their "Contact Us" page.

If you can't get social links added to your web site's template, you may want to think about adding them to your contact page. If you'd like to encourage supporters to reach out via these channels, adding them can be a quick win that will make your staff more available and further promote your social channels.

But don't stop at the contact page—there are plenty of other ways to integrate social channels in your organization's contact information. Here are a few more places where social links can be added to existing contact information:

- List social accounts in your web site's header or footer, typically as icons.
- Insert social links or icons on print ads, fliers, and direct mail pieces.
- Add Facebook and Twitter links to letterhead and other paper appeals.
- Place links to Facebook and Twitter at the end of donation, volunteer, and other transactional processes.
- Insert links, via graphics or hyperlinks, in the e-mail signatures of your staff.
- Add social links to your staff's business cards.

 Integrate Supporter Photos with Other Channels

Supporters of your organization are often the best people to tell your story. With the growing trend of photo and video sharing online, ask your supporters to help spread the word about your cause through images. Don't just gather the photos though, put them to work! By integrating supporter photos into other channels like your web site, your e-newsletters, and so on, you are not only lessening the amount of legwork you have to do to get artwork, but also communicating through your supporters.

What You Need A plan for using the photos, clear usage rules, a strong call to action, and a process for submitting them

How to Do It

1. Before you just start gathering photos for your organization's scrapbook, be sure you have a plan in place to display them.
2. Develop usage rules for every way you anticipate using the photos and display them clearly.
3. Get the word out! Create a call to action that encourages supporters to submit photos and provides easy instructions for how to do so.
4. Use the photos (with permission) in your e-newsletter, on your web site, on your Facebook page, in a tweet—the possibilities are endless!

A Closer Look   In an effort to inspire its supporters, the Sierra Club sends out an e-newsletter called the Daily Ray of Hope, which contains inspirational quotes and user-generated photos. The organization reaches out to its supporters for help in compiling inspiring nature photos that "remind people why we all work so hard to protect the natural environment, and that will give people a little extra pep in their step!"

The Sierra Club has made it easy for supporters to contribute by creating a Flickr group (see Tactic 16) called the Daily Ray of Hope group. The group has more than 1600 members and contains nearly 22,000 images. (Enough photos for 60 years!) The Daily Ray has about 6,900 subscribers, which is relatively modest for a national e-newsletter from Sierra Club, but boasts a 50 percent open rate, which is pretty high by comparison.

If staff chooses to include a particular image, the supporter is notified and credit is given alongside the photo. The organization also includes photos (with permission) on its social networks like Twitter and Facebook.

"The Daily Ray is a fan favorite, because it's one of the few e-newsletters we put out there in which we aren't asking them to take action or donate money or anything like that," says Brian Foley, Sierra

Since 1892, the Sierra Club (www.sierraclub.org) has been working to protect communities, wild places, and the planet itself and hails itself as the largest and most influential grassroots environmental organization in the United States.

Club's online media writer. "They're just nice pictures from people on Flickr accompanied by an uplifting quote—subscribers know exactly what they're getting. That's why the Daily Ray has such a high open rate."

 ## 38 Submit Content to Social News and Bookmarking Sites

Social news and bookmarking sites like Digg, Yahoo! Buzz, StumbleUpon, and Delicious can help bring your content to a new audience. It is easy to submit blog posts, news articles, photos, and videos as part of your marketing communications process, but it's also wise to encourage your supporters to share on your behalf. If your latest blog post has widespread appeal, having it hit the front page of Digg or Yahoo! Buzz can bring spikes in new visitors, memberships, and hopefully donations. That same content can live on forever in the StumbleUpon and Delicious communities, bringing a steady drip of new visitors over a long period of time. So share and share often, and encourage your supporters to do the same!

What You Need Personal accounts on social news and bookmarking sites, content to submit to these sites, a way to encourage your supporters to submit your content, and a web analytics tool for tracking

How to Do It

1. Get to know the community. If you are unfamiliar with the way social news and bookmarking sites work, create a personal account and participate. Take a close look at the type of content that does well, how the story titles are worded, and when they become popular.
2. Identify content to share. Determine which content of yours would appeal to these audiences, or create a plan to get some published. A blog is a great place to start.
3. Submit and monitor your content. Based on your knowledge of each community, submit posts that have the best chances of being promoted to the homepage. Pay close attention to each story's title, description, category, and submission time.

4. Help your supporters share your content. If you're sharing content from a blog or web site, make sure you have included tools to help visitors share on your behalf. Using widgets like ShareThis are effective and very easy to get installed (see Tactic 13).

5. Collect and analyze all the data you can! Getting all of this done can take some effort, so make sure it is worth it by tracking each story. Look at how it performed, what kind of traffic it brought to your web site, and whether those visitors took a meaningful action.

A Closer Look   Nonprofits that churn out amazing online content can get it in front of new audiences because of the way social news sites work. When a great blog post is submitted, viewed, and loved, it may hit the home page as a featured item. This will bring huge spikes in traffic to the web site or blog, consisting mostly of visitors new to the organization's message.

Producing content that will resonate on social news sites can be challenging, and is easier for certain types of nonprofits. Performing arts, environmental, animal rights, and political organizations can often produce media-rich posts that become popular, so a blog is a great place to start.

Danielle Brigida, digital marketing manager at The National Wildlife Federation, has widely shared her experiences using Digg. com to promote content for the Wildlife Promise blog. A typical post on Wildlife Promise would receive about 1,500 views per day, but would balloon to more than 45,000 views when a piece of content hit the front page of Digg. The majority of this traffic was new to NWF, and over time this helped increase awareness of its brand and mission.

It's important to note that the majority of these new visitors will not convert into donors, members, or volunteers, something that is confirmed by Danielle's own experience and data. Danielle says, "The visitors from social news sites like Digg were not our typical visitors and only a small percentage would take action or make a donation. A majority of the benefits came from the increased search engine rankings and the exposure, not necessarily the massive number of visitors."

With that said, getting your organization's brand in front of millions of eyes can easily be worth the effort over time. Be sure to keep track of your metrics on the social sites themselves (e.g., diggs, bookmarks, upvotes, likes, and comments), as well as the volume and type of traffic those sites are sending your way. Once you get a clear picture of what content is working, you'll know where to focus your attention.

 Create a Wikipedia Entry

Search for just about anything and chances are, Wikipedia will show up in the top 10 organic search results (if not as the first). If your organization has an entry on Wikipedia, you should regularly monitor it at the least; if it does not, you should consider creating one. To qualify for a Wikipedia entry, your organization must meet Wikipedia's relatively strict notability guidelines, which basically means that the topic (your organization) has received significant coverage in reliable independent sources and is "worthy of notice." If your organization isn't "notable" yet, start by working on that!

What You Need   A Wikipedia account, a notable (encyclopedia-worthy) subject, and third-party references to cite

How to Do It
1. Sign up for a free Wikipedia account. Learn the community's rules, and practice editing pages before jumping in.
2. Determine if your organization fits Wikipedia's notability requirements. If it doesn't, work on getting some news coverage, awards, and so on!
3. Gather your sources. You will need to cite third-party sources when writing your entry.
4. Create your entry. There are many resources on Wikipedia to help you along.
5. Encourage others to add to it and request feedback from the community—it is meant to be a collaborative effort.
6. Regularly monitor your entry to make sure that it is updated and error free.

A Closer Look   Manny Hernandez (@askmanny), president of Diabetes Hands Foundation (@diabetesHF) and social media blogger at

Askmanny.com shares the following tips for writing a Wikipedia entry for your nonprofit:

- Abide by the rules—become familiar with the Wikipedia community and dos and don'ts before you dive into editing pages.
- Contribute as much as you can to the entire Wiki—if you know anything about any topic, look for it on Wikipedia and find ways to improve articles.
- Be VERY critical of your organization's notability—be sure it aligns with Wikipedia's published requirements.
- Adhere to Wikipedia's Neutral Point of View style—keep it factual, sourced, and balanced.
- Be ready for a LOT of back-and-forth and for engaging in what could be a very long-term project. This potentially includes multiple edits and/or deletions. If your article gets deleted, really think it through as there is likely a good reason why it shouldn't be on Wikipedia, even if you think otherwise.

"If there is an existing Wikipedia page about your organization, it is very important that you monitor it and contribute to it as you would to any other Wikipedia page," says Manny.

 ## 40   Create a Social Media Newspaper

People are being hit with more and more messages in their social networks each day. So much so, that it is hard to find the information most important to them. Make it easy for supporters to follow and subscribe to the social media buzz around your cause by creating a paper.li newspaper. Paper.li aggregates Twitter and Facebook social media activity, hashtags, or Twitter lists and displays it as an online newspaper with topical sections. You can customize the paper to display updates based on advanced Twitter queries too.

What You Need A Twitter or Facebook account and a subject or hashtag to focus the paper on (optional)

How to Do It
1. Visit paper.li.
2. Sign up for an account by entering your Twitter or Facebook credentials.

3. When prompted, enter your e-mail address for updates about your paper.
4. Click "create a newspaper" in the upper right-hand corner of the site.
5. Select the type of paper you want to create. (The more specific you get, the more relevant and engaging it will be.)
6. Click "create," and the paper will be processed and updated every 24 hours. (As long as there are views every two days.)
7. You can choose to automatically promote your paper by clicking on the megaphone button. You can also encourage people to subscribe via e-mail by clicking the subscribe button. Be sure to add an editor's note that links back to your web site to personalize the paper.

A Closer Look   A great paper to read to get to know paper.li is The #nonprofit Daily. It aggregates news, blog posts, and multimedia from around the nonprofit world in the following categories: education, stories, business, art and entertainment, health, technology, #fundraising, and #charity. You can even browse the archives to see past papers.

Paper.li is now available in six languages and will soon unveil new branding and skinning functionality, as well as advanced curation and management features. The papers are so interactive that readers can hover over avatars below articles and choose to retweet, reply, favorite, follow, and unfollow directly from the article.

Once you create your paper, in order for it to automatically update daily, you must opt for the auto-promotion or be sure to visit it on a daily basis. If there are no page views for 48 hours, the paper will switch to a manual update mode where users have to press the "Update Paper Now" button.

The key is to strike a balance of marketing your paper without it being just another promotional message clogging up your organization's Twitter stream. You want this to be a value-add service for supporters, not just another channel to add to the pile.

41   Make a Buzzworthy Video

If a picture is worth 1000 words, well, then a video has to be worth at least a million. Think of the last video you remember watching . . . Did it make you laugh, blush, or cry? Chances are, if you remember it, it evoked some sort of deep emotion. In order for your video to be effective and create a buzz, it has to do the same. Don't make a boring video, make one that viewers will remember and share!

What You Need   An experienced videographer (you want it to be real, but not real as in shaking Blair Witch-style videos), decent video equipment, a good editor, and a striking idea

How to Do It

1. Gather a diverse group for a brainstorming session—you never know whose head that next brilliant idea is lurking in.
2. Determine what you are trying to achieve. Start with the call to action and work backward. What would lead your viewers to respond? Create a buzz!
3. Shoot and edit a brief compelling video. There are a lot of free nonprofit resources out there for stock images and music for use in your video (creativecommons.org, mobygratis.com) and volunteer-matching programs through YouTube and Lights, Camera, Help!—take advantage of them!
4. Use online and social media to promote it.

A Closer Look   For the 2009 Super Bowl, PETA created an advertisement in hopes of exposing football fans to vegetarianism. Well, it never ran during the game, but got a lot more bang for its buck via national news coverage and online. The ad, "Veggie Love," was banned from TV because of several scantily clad women who couldn't resist "veggie love." The idea behind the outrageous ad turned viral video was that vegetarians have better sex (see Exhibit 2.12).

What really increased the buzz was the rejection letter from NBC claiming that it was banned because of concerns over "rubbing pelvic region with pumpkin," a woman "screwing herself

People for the Ethical Treatment of Animals (PETA; www.peta.org) is the largest animal rights organization in the world, and focuses its attention on factory farms, in the clothing trade, in laboratories, and in the entertainment industry.

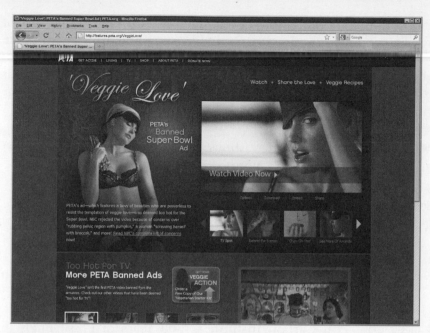

Exhibit 2.12   People for the Ethical Treatment of Animals' Veggie Love web site
Source: Courtesy of the People for the Ethical Treatment of Animals

with broccoli," and more. The response helped PETA get national press and millions of online views of the video. In total, it received more than 3.5 million views, a third of viewers went on to watch a more serious pro-vegetarian video called "Chew On This," and nearly 5,000 viewers went on to order free vegetarian starter kits after watching the video.

"The video was a huge success for PETA and achieved exactly what we had hoped—a fun video that grabbed people's attention, but then directed them to more serious content," says Amy Cook, PETA's marketing manager.

 Participate in a Video Contest

Each year, YouTube, in collaboration with See3 Communications, holds the "DoGooder Nonprofit Video Awards," which promotes the use of video by nonprofits. In 2011, there were 1350 entries and four winning organizations were featured on the homepage of YouTube and received grants and video equipment. The exposure your organization could get from winning this contest is unparalleled. And, if you're an odds person, the odds of winning this contest are pretty good (much better than simply wishing your video goes viral!).

What You Need   A great video showcasing your cause and a (free) membership in YouTube's Nonprofit Program

How to Do It
1. Apply to the YouTube Nonprofit Program.
2. Once the contest opens, submit your video entry at http:// youtube.com/nonprofitvideoawards.
3. You will receive an e-mail with a confirmation link, click it to finalize the submission.

A Closer Look   Post Carbon Institute's "300 Years of Fossil Fuels in 300 seconds" video won in the category of Best Small Organization Video in the 5th Annual DoGooder Nonprofit Video Awards held in 2011 (see Exhibit 2.13). Tod Brilliant, who manages PCI's strategy and communication says the video was crafted in an effort to succinctly tell the story of fossil fuels in society. Even though the contest was free and easy to enter, according to Tod, it has produced amazing returns.

As a winner of the DoGooder Nonprofit Video Awards, PCI received a Flip camera and a $2500 grant. After being featured on the homepage of YouTube, the video's views shot to 800,000 in 10 days with a healthy discussion of more than 4000 comments. (Typically, the organization's videos have about 1000 views.) In addition, PCI tripled the number of YouTube followers, added 1400

Post Carbon Institute (PCI; www.postcarbon.org) provides individuals, communities, businesses, and governments with the resources needed to understand and respond to the interrelated economy, energy, environmental, and equity crises that define the 21st century.

Exhibit 2.13   DoGooder Nonprofit Video Awards hope page
Source: Courtesy of YouTube

Facebook followers, and the video received an additional 15,000 shares on Facebook. The organization has also benefited from the exposure in more subtle ways through new partnerships, a boost in the sales of its book, *The Post Carbon Reader*, and, says Tod, "a whole lot of organizational pride. In our work, it's easy to get discouraged/depressed. The win really blew some air into our sails."

 ## Livestream Your Events

Producing live video is extremely accessible thanks to inexpensive equipment and web technology, which means it's easier than ever for nonprofits to make events available to distant supporters. Organizations are streaming their runs, walks, galas, auctions, gatherings, and other events to their supporters, as well as key stories and messages from their leadership, volunteers, and recipients. By using services like UStream.tv, you can easily set up a live show then use your Facebook and Twitter accounts to call your fans to tune in. Live video can bring your mission to far away supporters, and increases participation through live chat.

What You Need   An account with UStream.tv or similar service, a web camera, a Facebook page, and a Twitter account

How to Do It
1. Identify an event, presentation, or message you want to broadcast live.
2. Create an account at UStream.tv, and set up your channel.
3. Create a show, and test your settings.
4. Announce on Twitter and Facebook that your event is live

A Closer Look   If you have an event with an existing live component, such as a race, auction, or a-thon, streaming can enhance the experience and extend the reach of your audience.

When Kevin Kline, Snowdrop Foundation's president and co-founder, began a 13-day run from Dallas > Austin > San Antonio > Houston, it was called Strides Across Texas and broadcast live on Ustream.tv. Sean McCoy, executive board member at the Snowdrop Foundation, says, "We wanted to share Kevin's second-by-second journey during his 471-mile, 13-day ultramarathon across Texas, and UStream.tv was the perfect medium to do so in every respect."

This broadcast helped bring attention to the cause, extended the reach of the event, and was relatively simple to execute. Sean adds, "It was extremely easy to set up, and more importantly share with our viewers. A simple laptop, wifi, and webcam are all we needed to broadcast our event to the world."

If your nonprofit already has compelling video content, engaging events, or a dynamic public spokesperson, the jump

Snowdrop Foundation (www.snowdropfoundation.org) is dedicated to assisting patients and families at Texas Children's Cancer Center through funding for continued research to eliminate childhood cancer and scholarships for college-bound pediatric cancer patients and survivors.

to live video may be an easy one. Hosting scheduled, fireside chats with tools like Ustream.tv allow hosts to interact with an audience live via online chat. A pet shelter will find no shortage of cute things to stream, and a performing arts organization can broadcast an event live, but other nonprofits need to get creative.

Don't underestimate your supporters' desire for interesting and funny videos (see Tactic 39). If you have a fundraiser involving 200 remote control planes, one of those "polar bear" runs into freezing water, or a dunk tank, putting it live online can get your nonprofit lots of attention. An interesting live event announced via Twitter and Facebook can go viral in a matter of minutes.

 Provide Instant Access to Content with QR Codes

Getting supporters to take action is the goal of any campaign, and sometimes words can simply get in the way. Quick Response (QR) Codes are images that can link to online content by simply being scanned by a reader app on a smartphone. This is a fun, visual, and social way to link to content in an easy way—by removing the typing! QR codes can be scanned by a smartphone, and within a couple of seconds begin loading a welcome page, donation form, or list of volunteer opportunities. When compared to friendly URLs and SMS messaging, QR codes make it much easier for your message to be heard out in the field.

What You Need   Content to share, a QR code creator, a smartphone, a QR code reader, and a graphic designer for layout

How to Do It
1. Identify a key web page you want to link to—a donation form, a volunteer page, or a welcome message.
2. Paste the URL of that web page into a QR code generator, like kaywa.com, QRStuff.com, bit.ly, or goo.gl.
3. Download the QR code graphic that was generated by the tool.
4. Insert that QR code into a flier, poster, letter, or other printed material.

5. Download a QR code reader, like i-nigma, and perform a test scan to make sure the image is pointing to the right location.
6. Get the QR code out in front of your audience.
7. Measure your results using metrics from the QR code generator and web analytics tools.

A Closer Look When the Pancreatic Cancer Action Network was brainstorming ideas for an awareness event at an upcoming L.A. Kings game, QR codes were on the mind of Allison Nassour. The Pancreatic Cancer Action Network's social media manager had seen traditional calls to action become tired and felt that QR codes could attract more respondents. Most of the attendees at the game would be new to the organization and carrying smartphones, so she knew this would be a great chance to beta test the technology.

A handout was created containing two calls to action pointing to the organization's "Get Involved" page on its web site, which was then passed out to around 1000 Kings fans (see Exhibit 2.14). After the game, the results showed that over 200 people had scanned the QR code and only 30 people had used the text messaging component. Allison says, "The QR code had almost seven times as many respondents as the text to donate. I knew it was pretty significant, especially because the flier was competing with all other stimuli at the game."

QR codes are so easy to use because of their simplicity, and that's why they're so great to socialize on posters, handouts, business cards, and t-shirts. When asked about the future of QR codes at the Pancreatic Cancer Action Network, Allison says, "We're most likely going to be adding the codes to posters for our PurpleStride events, and encouraging people to scan the code to make donations, watch videos, and hopefully register." She's right, QR codes can make any call to action that much easier when you're on the go, so think about how you can use them at your next event.

The Pancreatic Cancer Action Network (www.pancan.org) is a nationwide network of people dedicated to working together to advance research, support patients and create hope for those affected by pancreatic cancer.

HERE'S WHY YOUR SUPPORT IS URGENTLY NEEDED:

- Pancreatic cancer is the fourth leading cause of cancer death in the U.S.

- This year, an estimated 43,140 people will be diagnosed with pancreatic cancer in the U.S., and approximately 36,800 will die from the disease.

- Seventy five percent of patients die within the first year of diagnosis.

- Pancreatic cancer is the only one of the top ten cancer killers with a five-year survival rate still in the single digits—and the survival rate hasn't changed in nearly 40 years.

- There are no early detection methods and few treatment options for pancreatic cancer. And there is no cure.

YOU can be a hero and help change these dire statistics.

Text 'Hero' to 30644 for information about the Pancreatic Cancer Action Network and to find out how you can be a hero in the fight against pancreatic cancer.

Snap this QR code with your cell phone to see how you can get involved!

If you do not have a QR code reader on your cell phone, go to the app store & search "QR Reader."

 PANCREATIC CANCER ACTION NETWORK®
ADVANCE RESEARCH. SUPPORT PATIENTS. CREATE HOPE.

Toll Free: 877-272-6226 | Phone: 310-725-0025 | www.pancan.org

Exhibit 2.14   The back of Pancreatic Cancer Action Network's event handout

Source: Courtesy of the Pancreatic Cancer Action Network

Share Presentations and Documents Online

When your nonprofit has great content, you want to share it—and that goes for PowerPoint presentations and documents as well. SlideShare.net has built a social community around uploaded presentations and documents, and provides a home for useful, shareable content. Not only is your uploaded content accessible to the public, the presentations can be embedded on web sites and blogs (similar to a YouTube video). In addition, you can make the file available for download, engage with supporters via comments, and improve your SEO.

What You Need   A SlideShare.net account and a presentation or document to share

How to Do It

1. Identify presentations and documents you want to share online.
2. Create an account at SlideShare.net if you do not already have one.
3. Log in to your SlideShare.net account and press the "Upload" button.
4. Enter a title, description, tags, and a category for the presentation.
5. Unmark the "Allow users to download file" checkbox if you want to restrict downloading. You can set the copyright information as well.
6. Press the "Save Details" button.
7. Once the presentation is published, you can modify all the information by clicking the "edit presentation" link.
8. Share the presentation on your web site or blog by using the provided embed code.

A Closer Look   There are many reasons why sharing a great presentation or document can be beneficial, and SlideShare.net provides a free, feature-rich environment where nonprofits can do so. An uploaded presentation can easily be shared, discussed, and embedded in a blog, then seen by tons of new people. It can also become a search engine optimization outpost pointing back to your main web site, improving your organic rankings.

Exhibit 2.15   NTEN's 2011 Nonprofit Technology Conference event page on SlideShare
Source: Courtesy of the Nonprofit Technology Network; SlideShare

When the NTEN was looking for a way to organize content from its annual NTC, SlideShare made a lot of sense (see Exhibit 2.15). Anna Richter, NTEN's program director, says, "Collecting the presentations in one *central* place online allows us to share them with NTC attendees and non-attendees alike. For the presentations we are able to place online prior to the conference, it allows attendees to follow along during sessions on their laptops or to print out materials on their own to take notes. Post-event, we point folks to SlideShare as one of the places they can go and see what was presented at the NTC."

The flexibility of the platform allows NTEN to create an event page where speakers can upload their own presentations, preserving ownership for the content creators. This makes it easy for their audience to find the presentations, consume the content, and share it with their peers. And while getting these presentations in front of NTEN's audience is key, Anna shared, "Anecdotally, we will get folks interested in the NTC and NTEN because they have stumbled across a presentation from the conference on SlideShare."

3

Engage

Every nonprofit wants an active and engaged base from which to draw support. From the moment someone first learns about your nonprofit, each action is a step forward in the relationship—steps taken together for a greater purpose. Creating these opportunities is what social media engagement, and this chapter, are all about.

The previous chapter discussed how clear communication is the key to awareness, and you learned how nonprofits are sharing their missions with new and existing supporters. Now it's time to get your supporters tweeting, sharing, commenting, blogging, filming, and photographing your mission. The tactics in this chapter will help take your nonprofit's communication to the next level by encouraging supporters to get involved and take action.

Social media engagement is one of the best ways to get supporters hooked on your mission or further entrench them if they're already fans. Every action they take on your behalf or interaction they have with your staff pushes them closer and closer to becoming a lifelong supporter who donates, joins, or volunteers.

And the best part of social media engagement is how each action is seen throughout the network. Getting a supporter to take an action, "like" something, or post a comment increases the chances that one of his or her friends will see the activity and want to learn more. We call this "feeding the feed," and an engaged fan will help spread your message far and wide each time they take an action.

Create a Facebook Welcome Tab

A lifetime of engagement begins with a first impression, and for many nonprofit supporters this initial encounter occurs on Facebook. Creating a custom welcome tab gives Facebook visitors a clear picture of your organization, its mission, and how they can help (e.g., register for a newsletter, sign a petition, or volunteer). This calling card provides a better snapshot of your cause than the wall, and the page's settings can be changed to have visitors land there first. Make it count, as you never get another chance to make a first impression!

What You Need A Facebook page, a web host, and a designer for graphics and layout

How to Do It
1. Design the welcome tab content. Include your organization's name, logo, key messages, and a clear call to action. Ask them to like your page too!
2. Build the HTML file that will be your welcome tab. Facebook uses iFrames to pull in this HTML file as the custom tab. Facebook tabs have a maximum width of 520 pixels wide, so make sure that the page layout can fit in that amount of space.
3. Put the HTML file and any supporting files on your web server (e.g., images, style sheets, scripts), and note the URL.
4. Visit http://developers.facebook.com and click on "Apps" in the upper right-hand corner.
5. If you have not already authorized the developer app, sign in and follow the instructions.
6. In the upper right-hand corner, press "Create New App" (you may need to verify your account at this point).
7. Name your app, agree to Facebook's terms (if you do), and complete the security check.
8. Complete the "Basic Info" section, including uploading an icon and setting the app domain.
9. Complete the Facebook integration section by completing the "App on Facebook" and "Website" subsections, then save your changes.

10. Click on "View App Profile Page" on the left-hand side.
11. Click on "Add to My Page" on the left-hand side. Select the page you would like to add it to.
12. Visit the Application Profile Page of the custom app you just created (the link is on the right side of the app's listing on the Facebook Developers site), and click "Add to My Page" in the left navigation.
13. Visit your organization's page to ensure the tab is displaying properly.
14. If you want visitors to land on the welcome tab, click the "Edit Page" button on your organization's page and change the "Default Landing Tab" to the new welcome tab.

A Closer Look   The first goal of your organization's Facebook page is to get a visitor to like it. Having someone land on a welcome tab is one of the best ways to convert them to a fan. BrandGlue's May 2010 study showed that page conversions can be as high has 47 percent when using a welcome tab,[1] so this is one tactic that shouldn't be overlooked.

Designing a welcome tab that introduces your nonprofit and encourages people to like your page is the primary objective. Getting things set up in Facebook is relatively easy, so most of the effort involves designing the tab's layout and message.

Think about how to quickly tell visitors what your nonprofit is all about and how they can get started. Your mission statement or tagline will both work, but also include some language that prompts visitors to like your page. That is the action you want them to take first, and then it's okay to use the tab to point to other key content areas, like your wall, web site, blog, programs, or featured campaign.

Here are the Facebook welcome tabs of five organizations you can look to for inspiration:

- Oxfam GB uses a welcome tab that includes links to all of its other Facebook content and a form to sign up for the newsletter. www.facebook.com/oxfamGB

---

[1] Eric Eldon, "Facebook Creates, Removes Restriction on Landing Page Tabs," Inside Facebook, May 20th, 2010, http://www.insidefacebook.com/2010/05/20/facebook-creates-removes-restriction-on-landing-page-tabs.

- The Nature Conservancy has a welcome tab featuring a beautiful Like Box enticing visitors to become a fan. This is followed by key actions the user can take, like "Join The Cause" and "Post To Wall." www.facebook.com/thenature conservancy
- The YWCA USA welcome tab is clean, simple, and effective (see Exhibit 3.1). It features a photo of several women all pointing to the Like Button with a caption of "Own the Future. Like the Page!" www.facebook.com/pages/YWCA-USA/127821707877
- Greenpeace USA simply displays its mission with a "Click Like to join Greenpeace" call to action. www.facebook.com/greenpeaceusa
- The Canadian Opera Company begins its welcome tab with an offer, "Like our Facebook page for an exclusive coupon for any spring performance!" This is followed by a photo calendar of upcoming performances. www.facebook.com/canadianoperacompany

Exhibit 3.1   YWCA's Facebook welcome tab

Source: Courtesy of YWCA-USA; Facebook

Encourage Action with Facebook Custom Tab

You already know visitors to your Facebook page "like" your organization; why not give them the chance to get further involved by taking an action? Creating a custom tab on Facebook gives supporters a place to take their engagement to the next level. There are multiple ways you can go about this tactic—two of the most popular are marketing one call to action on its own tab and marketing multiple calls to action on one tab.

What You Need   A Facebook page, a web server, and a web developer

How To Do It   See tactic 46 for instructions on how to create a custom tab.

A Closer Look   Best Friends Animal Society (BFAS) puts Facebook custom tabs to work by incorporating specific calls to action on their own tabs. The organization also uses Facebook to drive visitors to its e-commerce site, among other promotions.

Best Friend's Kanab, Utah, headquarters is home to the largest no-kill sanctuary for homeless companion animals, and the organization has about 2000 animals in need of homes at any given time. Since adoption is core to the organization's mission, social media staffers created an "Adopt Me!" tab and placed it prominently on the page (see Exhibit 3.2). The tab features two pets of the week and links to even more adoptable pets, all within the tab. The branding matches the look and feel of the web site so the transition is seamless for visitors who click through. And, the organization can link directly to the tab when referring people to it in its other channels.

"The Adopt Me! tab provides a very positive way for us to showcase our animals," says Jon Dunn, BFAS' senior manager of online strategy. "Each animal receives scores of clicks each week—sometimes

Best Friends Animal Society's (www.bestfriends.org) mission is to bring about a time when there are No More Homeless Pets. The organization demonstrates and promotes exemplary animal care and builds community programs and partnerships.

Exhibit 3.2   Best Friends Animal Society's "Adopt Me!" Facebook custom tab
Source: Courtesy of Best Friends Animal Society; Facebook

numbering in the hundreds. We have seen adoptions of our animals because of the profile they receive as a 'Pet of the Week.'"

Another alternative is to simply create a custom tab that aggregates multiple calls to action. The tab should be its own call to action, that is, "Get Involved," featuring ways to sign up for a newsletter, donate to the organization, purchase goods, and the like.

48   Encourage Supporters to Share Facebook Content

Posting content on your organization's wall (see Tactic 9) gives your supporters a convenient way to consume it on Facebook. This ease of use can also be exploited when trying to expand the reach of your Facebook updates by encouraging fans to share them with their own networks. When one of your Facebook fans clicks the share button under a wall post or photo, that content will be posted to their own wall. If done tactfully, asking your Facebook network for help is an effective way to spread your message fast.

What You Need   A Facebook page and some good content to share

How to Do It

1. Using Facebook Insights, identify previously posted content that has performed well on your organization's page.
2. The next time you post similar content, or have an important update you'd like new people to see, add a "Please share this with your friends" statement.
3. Alternatively, you can remind your Facebook fans to share your content by writing a wall post or sending an update.

A Closer Look   Getting Facebook fans to share content should be top of mind, and the platform is literally built to help accomplish this. Publishing engaging blog content, interesting videos, and beautiful photos is the easiest way to get people to share with their network, but it doesn't hurt to ask from time to time either.

Tina Arnoldi, director of information management at the Coastal Community Foundation of SC, says "I think there's no harm in asking as long as it's not desperate sounding, or done constantly. If it's occasional, or is something like the Chase Community Giving Program, people who love you can support you with little effort."

An alternative to asking is to tie sharing and other actions into a promotion. Joe Waters, founder and blogger at Selfishgiving.com, shares, "A great way for nonprofits to get Facebook users to share wall posts is to launch a cause-marketing promotion. That's what Second Harvest Food Bank in San Mateo, California did with corporate partner Massage Envy. The company agreed to make a donation when users liked the page, commented, or posted a picture showing their support. It worked! The promotion galvanized fans of the food bank and Massage Envy donated $15,000 to the charity." This makes sense; supporters get involved and take action when they know there is a financial benefit for their favorite organization.

The bottom line is that if your nonprofit has great content, the network effect of Facebook will help it reach a new audience. John Haydon, chief heretic and pyrotechnician at Inbound Zombie, says, "There are countless tactics that nonprofits can use to encourage more sharing within Facebook, but the most important factor is that the content itself has to be absolutely stellar. It should be truly worth sharing." Once you have the content, it never hurts to encourage your fans to help out, so just ask.

49   Launch a Like Campaign

A core goal in your social media strategy (you have one of those, right? If not, see Tactic 101) should be to grow your organization's presence and reach. Acquiring new supporters is expensive. However, with Facebook, there are many tools and techniques to help you connect with potential supporters. If Facebook advertising is not in your budget, consider launching a "like" campaign. By relying on your existing supporters to recruit their friends, you will benefit from the viral nature of Facebook without spending a penny.

What You Need   A Facebook page with an existing supporter base and a great call to action

How To Do It

1. Be direct. Just ask! Periodically reach out to supporters in a status update saying "Since you like our page, help us grow by sharing it with your friends via the share link in the lower left corner."
2. From the share link, there are a variety of ways supporters can share your page: on their own wall, on a friend's wall, in a group, or in a private message. Your supporters may not know how, walk them through it!
3. Set a goal and go for it. Ask each supporter to recruit one of their friends to the page in honor of a special event or campaign (i.e., breast cancer awareness month).
4. Use all marketing vehicles at your disposal; extend the campaign by using e-mail, Twitter, LinkedIn, and newsletters.

A Closer Look   When 220 of California's 278 state parks were faced with massive state funding cuts, the California State Parks Foundation (CSPF) launched a multichannel effort to raise awareness and advocate the issue.

The California State Parks Foundation (www.calparks.org) is the only statewide independent nonprofit organization dedicated to protecting, enhancing, and advocating for California's state parks.

CSPF launched a "Friend Get a Friend" campaign on Facebook via the following update to 517 fans: "This year's cuts are 10 times as bad, so we need 10 times the fans on Facebook." Well, the organization didn't end up with 10 times as many fans, but nearly 64 times as many![2]

In two weeks, with just one more update and by leveraging other existing marketing outreach, the organization grew from 517 fans to 33,000. This show of support provided a case for keeping the parks funded and even got the Foundation coverage in major media outlets. They now have more than 60,000 fans.

"Not only did a severe crisis lend itself to timely and important messaging—there was a real hunger for info about what was really happening with state parks—but it was also teamwork," says Jerry Emory, CSPF's director of communications. "The president of CSPF recognized the opportunity and basically said "'Go for it!'"

Jerry and his team partnered with Brenna Holmes from Adams Hussey and Associates (now Chapman Cubine Adams + Hussey) to manage the early phenomenal growth of the page. CSPF now manages its Facebook presence in-house (but still receives feedback and ideas from its consultant) and has settled into a more planned management of the site. He adds, "We can still move quickly, and we are always innovating, but we also have a basic schedule for our postings now."

As California's budget continues to get cut, further threatening park closures, the organization now turns to its massive supporter base on Facebook to drive traffic to its advocacy site, which encourages supporters to take action by e-mailing their state representative.

 ## Use Facebook as Your Organization's Page

Facebook's "Use Facebook as Page" functionality allows your organization to engage with other pages, helping you reach new supporters and build affinity. While using Facebook as your organization, you can like the pages of other nonprofits, companies, and places you have an association with. Once connected with these pages, you can interact with them on your organization's behalf

---

[2]Daniel Burstein, "Facebook Case Study: From 517 to 33,000 fans in two weeks (plus media coverage)," MarketingExperiments Blog, May 26, 2010, http://www.marketingexperiments.com/blog/research-topics/facebook.html.

through wall updates, comments, and likes, spreading the visibility of your own page. You can truly "be" your brand!

What You Need   A Facebook account and other Facebook pages that you like

How to Do It
1. Visit your organization's Facebook page.
2. Click "Use Facebook as [name of page]" in the Admins panel on the right.
3. Visit pages you have an affinity with, and press the Like Button.
4. When appropriate, leave wall posts, comments, and likes on these pages.

A Closer Look   As a nonprofit, posting and commenting on your own Facebook page's wall makes sense as an engagement strategy—it's a way to connect directly with your supporters. Facebook also allows your organization's page to engage as itself, on other pages. This puts your nonprofit's brand out in the community, contributing to the conversation.

Using Facebook as your organization's page takes some thought, because liking another page is essentially an endorsement, so be strategic. Find pages, groups, brands, and partners that can help support your mission, then slowly begin to communicate as your nonprofit's page.

Here are some ways different nonprofits can use this Facebook feature:

- Human Rights—resources, information, volunteer opportunities, and ways to give can all be left as updates on key Facebook pages during times of crisis and natural disasters.
- Environmental—updates can be posted on pages dealing with key issues, political figures, or causes.
- Animal Rights—messages can be left for celebrities and partners that help advocate on the organization's behalf.
- Higher Education—special acknowledgements can be left on pages related to the university, key donors, or the academic field in general.
- Arts & Cultural—theaters can leave posts on the pages of visiting artists and museums can make updates on pages related to historical topics.

- K-12 Schools—posts can be left on local pages to support fundraisers, student initiatives, athletic programs, and so on.

 ## Ask Your Facebook Fans a Question

Engagement is all about getting supporters to take an action that contributes to your mission, and sometimes that can simply be answering a question. Facebook makes it easy for nonprofits to pose a question to their fan base. This can be done by simply writing a question on your organization's Facebook wall, setting up a Facebook Questions poll, or posting an inquiry on your Twitter account. Whatever way, your supporters will feel more engaged when they are able to give you feedback on your programs, key issues, and thoughts on the future.

What You Need   A Facebook page

How to Do It
1. Determine a topic that your nonprofit would like feedback on. A recent event, key issue, fundraising program, volunteer opportunity, or other mission-related subject will work.
2. Visit your organization's Facebook wall, type the question, and press the "Share" button. To use Facebook Questions, click the "Question" link to get started.
3. Monitor the responses and provide appropriate feedback. The goal here is to engage, so don't be shy!
4. Post an update thanking everyone for participating, but also provide some insight into the answers given.

A Closer Look   Reaching out to your supporters for direct feedback can increase engagement by making them feel closer to your organization. Their thoughts and opinions are important, and social media is a great way to help them be heard.

Questions can be about anything, but try to keep them related to your mission. Making them short with clear answers will increase participation, especially if your supporters know they will see the results. Participation is the foundation of engagement, and asking for feedback is a great way to get the ball rolling.

Feeding America reaches out to its supporters for input on things like annual planning. The organization received a lot of ideas when it asked, "We are creating plans for our next fiscal year across the organization. Here is your chance to participate—what do you want to see on this Facebook page in the upcoming year? How can we engage you more?"

The Nonprofit Technology Network (NTEN) also does a great job of asking questions on its Facebook wall. NTEN has asked questions like, "Does 'IT' have its own department at your organization?," "What topic do you want to see us cover next?," and "Does anyone foresee a time when the traditional "Communications" role will be supplanted by what we now call "Community Manager" for nonprofit organizations?" These mission-related questions received a lot of feedback and helped keep their members involved with the organization.

And if you're looking for lots of interaction, ask something controversial. Amnesty International did this when they asked their Facebook fans, "Does the killing of Osama Bin Laden set a bad precedent? Will it make assassination politically acceptable for other countries as well?" More than 200 people responded, and this helped drive a conversation that was important to supporters.

 Get Creative with Avatars

What better way to spread your message than to provide your supporters with tools to do it themselves? By asking supporters to customize their avatar in support of a campaign, you are not only gaining their support, but also spreading awareness throughout their networks. There are many (free) tools that you can use to create avatar overlays; however, Twibbon.com provides the most comprehensive service that includes Facebook and Twitter integration.

What You Need   A Facebook or Twitter account, a campaign, and artwork

How to Do It
1. Visit http://twibbon.com and click "Start a Campaign."
2. Sign in via Facebook or Twitter.
3. Complete the form with basic information about the campaign.
4. Upload a 200 × 200 pixel image no larger than 150 kb to use for your Twibbon (you can either make a Twibbon online in one of two styles or upload your own).

5. There are many advanced options to customize the campaign for a fee, or you can choose the free option to create your campaign.

6. Market your campaign!

A Closer Look   In support of WWF's Earth Hour (wwf.org.uk/earth-hour) that took place at 8:30 P.M. on March, 26, 2011, WWF-UK invited supporters to add an overlay to their social media avatars. By adding a frame around their avatar with the signature WWF panda and the words "Earth Hour" at the bottom, participants showed their support of the campaign that aimed to tackle climate change and protect the natural world (see Exhibit 3.3).

> As part of the international WWF network, WWF-UK (www.wwf.org.uk) addresses global threats to people and nature such as climate change, the peril to endangered species and habitats, and the unsustainable consumption of the world's natural resources.

Exhibit 3.3   WWF-UK's Twibbon page
Source: Courtesy of WWF-UK; Twibbon

WWF-UK used Twibbon as a platform for the social media campaign. When people opted to support the cause, their avatar was overlaid with a WWF Twibbon. WWF-UK opted to upgrade to a custom campaign, so when people supported the cause, a tweet was posted from their account stating: "Support WWF's Earth Hour, add an #earthhour twibbon to show you care about tackling climate change! http://twb.ly/id9COQ." By participating, supporters also auto-followed @wwf_uk.

In just a few weeks, nearly 700 people showed their support of the cause by adding the Twibbon to their avatar, increasing awareness for the campaign, and increasing the organization's Twitter following.

 ## Add a Tweet Button to Your Web Site or Blog

Tweeting links to great content is something a lot of nonprofit supporters are already doing on their own, so why not make it easy for them to tweet your content? Giving readers a one-click option for tweeting content, like blog posts, team fundraising pages, or helpful resources, helps capitalize on the viral nature of social media. It only takes a few minutes to add a "Tweet This" button to your web site or blog template, and this can increase engagement with and affinity for your mission by making it easy for supporters to share your content with their own network.

What You Need   A Twitter account, the Twitter Tweet Button code, access to your web site or blog's files

How to Do It
1. Visit www.twitter.com/about/resources and click "Create Tweet Button."
2. Choose the style of button that fits into your web site or blog's layout.
3. Click the "Tweet Text" tab if you want the tweet to be something other than the title of the web page or blog.
4. The URL and Language tabs allow further customizations to the Button.

5. Add an optional Twitter account to be @replied in the tweet. Including your organization's handle here is a great way to increase exposure.

6. Copy and paste the generated code into your web site or blog's template, and test the results.

7. The Sharing API can be used to create custom versions of this button.

A Closer Look   Helping readers tweet content can be done via widgets like AddThis (see Tactic 14), but displaying the Twitter button itself makes it even easier for the sharing to happen. This button has become commonplace in blog layouts, and readers are accustomed to using them. If you don't include a Tweet Button, you've lost an excellent opportunity to help supporters spread the word.

Twitter's Tweet Button is widely used, and can be added in minutes. This button can be seen on many blogs as a standalone item, or as part of a more robust plug-in like World Vision uses on its blog. The TweetMeme retweet button is an alternative to using the native Twitter button, and can be seen on the Salvation Army blog. These buttons are easy to see and click, helping supporters spread the word.

Once you've decided to use the button on your blog, implementation becomes key. You want to display the button in a place visitors can easily see and use. Here are several ways to make your button more effective:

- Place the button near the title of the page or blog post, as this is the place most visitors will look for the button.
- Leave a good margin around the button to help it stand out—you won't want it to blend in to the content of the page.
- Put a duplicate copy of the button near the bottom of a blog post, between the final paragraph and the comments. This will help those who have scrolled to the bottom tweet the content.
- Make sure it isn't competing with a bunch of other social sharing tools.
- Monitor the button over time to see how often it is being used. Based on these observations and feedback from your readers, continue to adjust the placement of the button until you are happy with its performance.

54   Empower Supporters to Take Social Action

Supporters often want to take social actions on behalf of nonprofits, but sometimes need an extra push to get it done. If you're running a campaign or initiative that encourages supporters to tweet, leave Facebook updates, or blog, providing tools to make this easier can really increase participation. Create a web page that provides sample tweets and Facebook updates, related hashtags, scripts, statistics, and blog post topics. Giving supporters a little help getting started can go a long way toward spreading your message and fighting for your cause.

What You Need   A campaign, initiative, or program to rally supporters around and a web page to provide content

How to Do It

1. Identify an initiative that requires your supporters to take social action.
2. Determine what hashtags are being actively used around this cause (see Tactic 28). If none are being used, create your own.
3. Write a few sample tweets and Facebook updates that your supporters can use, including links. If you have an active blogging community, provide sample copy, quotes, and images that can be used.
4. Create a page on your web site that lists these hashtags, tweets, updates, and other information. Make it easy to scan so visitors can find what they need fast.
5. Promote the page in e-mails, social channels, and on your web site.
6. Monitor the discussion and modify your sample content based on what you learn.

A Closer Look   When it's time to call your army into action, it helps to give them a little training before sending them out into the field. When the United States was deep in a national discussion around the American Clean Energy and Security Act of 2009, The Environmental Defense Action Fund decided to help their supporters by creating a page called, "Twitter: A Guide to the Climate Bill Discussion" (see Exhibit 3.4).

The Environmental Defense Action Fund (www.edf.org) is the lobbying arm of Environmental Defense Fund, a leading environmental organization dedicated to educating the public about sound environmental policy and promoting lasting solutions to protect the environmental rights of all people.

This page contained all the information necessary to help supporters of The Environmental Defense Action Fund bring awareness to the climate legislation debate. The page begins by listing hashtags that supporters of the climate bill are using (e.g., #climatebill and #ACES), but also lists hashtags used by opponents of the bill (e.g., #capandtax and #tcot).

The page continues by providing example tweets that supporters can use to help the cause. The tweets are organized like a script, providing updates that can be used as rebuttals to opposing views. These pre-scripted tweets include a bit.ly link that EDF can track

Exhibit 3.4 Environmental Defense Fund's "Twitter: A Guide to the Climate Bill Discussion" web page

Source: Courtesy of Environmental Defense Action Fund at www.edf.org/page.cfm?tagID=45878; Twitter

(see Tactic 54), and also a "tweet this" link that will place the copy in Twitter for the user.

Lauren Guite, EDF's social media and marketing coordinator, says, "We came up with the idea to create what we call 'pre-tweets' to give our side some ammo. It ended up working pretty well, as it gave the average EDF supporter all the knowledge and confidence they needed to speak up in the debate. It also helped focus our messaging."

Making it easy for your supporters to take action is important if you want high participation. Creating a guide that focuses on social actions will help you help your supporters help the cause!

 Build Real Relationships with Social Communication

Social media has given nonprofits unprecedented access into the personal lives of supporters, and allows relationships to develop at a much quicker pace. These relationships are the foundation of every nonprofit, so using Twitter and Facebook to communicate with supporters can help keep a larger base engaged. Using these social platforms to reply, retweet, like, share, and interact with supporters will help relationships blossom into something more meaningful down the road.

What You Need   A Twitter account and Facebook page

How to Do It

1. Actively monitor each social channel for questions and comments being directed at your organization. You can use search. twitter.com to monitor important keywords and hashtags (see Tactic 96).
2. Determine the appropriate response and reply to the original person in a timely manner. Be sensitive to privacy issues and offer to take the conversation offline if need be.
3. Add each person you interact with to an influencer list, and try to track their level of engagement over time.
4. Evaluate the effort and create a formal response plan. This plan will reduce response time and help your program expand beyond a single staff member.

A Closer Look Building real relationships with mothers is something March of Dimes has always been about. For 15 years, March of Dimes has used its online question and answer portal to help mothers in need of help, and this same concept was extended in 2007 when Beverly Robertson, March of Dimes' national director at the Pregnancy & Newborn Health Education Center, created the @marchofdimes Twitter account (see Exhibit 3.5).

March of Dimes (www.marchofdimes.com) helps moms have full-term pregnancies and research the problems that threaten the health of babies.

March of Dimes began interacting on Twitter, "to talk to pregnant women (dads too) about their pregnancies, answer questions, provide information, and offer comfort when needed," Beverly says. "In short, we need to be relevant to people's lives. When asked 'What have you done for me lately?' I want that to be an easily

Exhibit 3.5   March of Dimes Twitter page
Source: ©March of Dimes Foundation, 2001. All rights reserved; Twitter

answered question. March of Dimes has answered my question. They provided me with information. They helped me when I was in crisis, when I had a baby in the NICU."

In a world where online marketing is always looking to get something out of you, this "audience-first" mindset has helped March of Dimes truly become a trusted source and seem more human. Beverly described those who reach out to @marchofdimes as, "Pleased, grateful, often surprised, and even shocked." She adds, "I used to get responses asking if I was the real March of Dimes. People do not expect to get a response in real time to comments or questions."

While it may be difficult to measure this type of engagement, turning a social media fan into a lifelong supporter is priceless. When asked how building real relationships benefits March of Dimes, Beverly says, "I know my followers. I remember if they have had a baby, a loss, or have volunteered for us. I know their interests and concerns. I check in on them, I rejoice with them, I thank them. I ask them to help raise awareness, to blog for us, to walk for us. And they do." That's as real as it gets!

 ## 56 Ask Influencers to Share Your News

Believe it or not, not everyone will see every tweet you beautifully craft—and it's just getting noisier and noisier in the Twitterverse as everyone's parents are joining the party. So, if you really want your organization's influencers and biggest supporters to see your news (and share it with their networks), tell them about it, and ask them to share it with their followers and friends. There is nothing wrong with giving them a heads-up, or in Twitter-speak, a dm (direct message) or @reply at the end of the tweet to make sure it gets on their radar. This not only helps your message spread further, but by reaching out to your influencers and asking them to take action, you are also engaging them and bringing them closer to your organization. You want to be sure and use this tactic sparingly—only for the really good stuff!

What You Need Compelling content, a Twitter or Facebook account, and a list of influencers with contact information

How to Do It

1. Know your influencers.
2. Like them, follow them, get to know them, and interact with them on a regular basis. This may seem contrived, but odds are, if they are influential to your organization, you probably genuinely will care about what they have to say. A retweet or a comment on a blog post means more than you think.
3. Tailor your pitch. Once you have compelling content that you are trying to get out there, take a look at the list and see who would care the most and have the most impact.
4. Consider "advancing" them the news or letting them in on it a day or two early.
5. When the news is posted, message them on Twitter or Facebook or e-mail them, giving them a heads-up and asking them to share it with their networks.

A Closer Look What's the best way to find your organization's influencers? It's easy to find your top donors or volunteers, but finding those most influential in spreading your message is a bit trickier. You can't look at giving history or hours volunteered, or even number of followers in this case (even though that can be one piece of the puzzle).

The best way to find them is to become part of the community you are trying to reach. The closer you are to the message and the more authentic it is, the more likely the community will be to care about it and take action.

The best place to start is by building a list of people by subject area or by geography. For example, if you are trying to reach greenies in Ohio, you may want to build a list of green blogs that are read in the Midwest. Then, next time you have an issue that needs their attention, you know who to reach out to.

Another great way to get your message out is through the media—and social media is a great way to reach them! Don't stop there though; build a list of politicians, celebrities, friends, and fans who are influential to your cause. You can come up with this list manually through research and by asking those close to the topic in question, or by using advanced monitoring platforms (like Vocus or mBLAST) to help you identify your top influencers.

Engage the Blogging Community

With their real-time, interactive, and personal nature, blogs have become one of the most powerful platforms for storytelling. By reaching out to your organization's existing blogger community and by forming relationships with key bloggers who are writing about your cause, when it comes time to spread the word about a timely issue or campaign, you will have a great network for helping you do so.

What You Need   Social platforms like Flickr, Twitter, Facebook, and YouTube, staff time for Internet research (or advanced monitoring platforms like mBLAST), and a web developer for site integration

How to Do It

1. Identify influential bloggers who align with your mission (see Tactic 57).
2. Introduce them to your organization's mission through a site visit or tour so they can experience your work first hand and possibly become an advocate for your cause.
3. Give them tools to spread the message beyond their blogs.
4. Encourage bloggers to use free tools like Twitter, Facebook, and YouTube to report from the scene.
5. Setup a landing page, hashtags, and Flickr pools to centralize content.
6. Provide a badge for the bloggers to display on their blog or their site to drive more traffic to your site, or to raise awareness for an issue.

A Closer Look   Each year, 8.1 million children under the age of five die. In 2010, Save the Children UK took three of the UK's top "mummy bloggers" on an inspirational adventure to Bangladesh to see firsthand and raise awareness of the scale of child mortality

Save the Children UK's (www.savethechildren.org.uk) mission is to inspire breakthroughs in the way the world treats children and to achieve immediate and lasting change in their lives.

in developing countries. Passionate about the organization's work, the bloggers tweeted, created video and photo galleries, and wrote about their experiences in Bangladesh.

The mums have already created a storm in the digital world talking about #blogladesh. They took this a step further by arranging meetings with Nick Clegg, the United Kingdom's deputy prime minister, to spread the message about Save the Children's initiatives. More than 10 million people have read and/or retweeted their blog posts and tweets, and 63,569 actions were taken towards increasing awareness of the health crisis (see Exhibit 3.6).

Liz Scarff, digital media consultant for Save the Children who devised and implemented the project says "Real change happens when people come together. #Blogladesh is Save the Children recognizing the power of social media and the value of working with external people as ambassadors. We're passionate about saving children's lives and mummy bloggers can link with that emotionally just by being who they are."

Exhibit 3.6   Save The Children UK's web site
Source: Courtesy of Save The Children UK

Scarff replicated and multiplied the success of #Blogladesh with the recent #Passiton project where she took three mums to follow the journey of a vaccine in Mozambique from a warehouse right down to a rural clinic. "We reached over 27 million people on Twitter, had hundreds of people and children blogging for us, managed to get meetings with government and Bill Gates, and the vaccine summit that we were raising awareness of had more money pledged than the target," she says.

58   Broadcast the Backchannel Buzz at Your Event

While there is a lot to be said for actually paying attention in class (conference, event, etc.), it is equally, if not more informative, to read and participate in the backchannel conversation. The backchannel is the stream of real-time conversation that is occurring live from the event. By creating a specific hashtag (see Tactic 26) and using a free tool like Visible Tweets or Twitterfall, you can broadcast the backchannel of the feed at the event, encouraging attendees to participate and see their tweet.

What You Need   A hashtag or search term and a broadcast setup (either a digital screen or a projector and wall)

How to Do It
1. Determine the hashtag you would like to use (see Tactic 26).
2. Select the broadcast service you would like to use (for this example, we will use Visible Tweets).
3. Visit Visibletweets.com and enter the hashtag or search term you would like to display.
4. Press "Go Full Screen" and the updates will automatically run.
5. If you choose to use monitors, place them in high-traffic areas. You can also project the feed onto a white screen or wall at the event.

A Closer Look   If you are encouraging backchannel conversation, you need to be sure that your event has free wifi access. Those using laptops or tablets will appreciate it.

Here are some tips for making the most of the backchannel at your event:

- Display it loud and proud—be sure your Twitter broadcast is large and noticeable. You will see that it is a sure traffic stopper and a nice backdrop in an auditorium setting. Large flat screen monitors near the entrance of the event or in a lounge area add to the excitement (see Exhibit 3.7).
- Encourage attendees to provide feedback about the event—you will often glean much more honest information than on post-event surveys.
- Be sure to have someone on your event staff monitoring the conversation so he or she can answer questions (how do I pay for my auction item?) and respond to feedback (this is the best event ever!) in real time.
- If you have a speaker at your event, have attendees submit questions by using the event hashtag and have a "Twitter moderator" feed them to the speaker.
- Hold a contest or a tweetaway! Even though Facebook has strict rules around contests (see Tactic 65), Twitter is still fair game (local laws do apply).

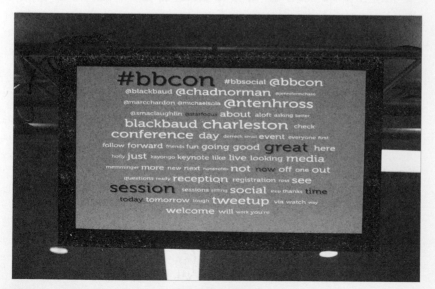

Exhibit 3.7   Photograph of live tweets on an LCD monitor
Source: Courtesy of Chad Norman

• Be sure to capture all of the action around the event hashtag by setting up a Twapperkeeper (visit Twapperkeeper.com).

59 Organize a Twitter Chat with a Hashtag

People love to chat, so setting up a chat tied to a hashtag can really get your Twitter crowd engaged. Twitter hashtags are effective at organizing conversations (see Tactic 26), and offer supporters an opportunity to learn something new, share what they already know, and meet new people—pretty much everything Twitter is about. Hosting a chat on Twitter will help get people more involved with your mission and demonstrate your nonprofit's leadership to the community.

What You Need   A Twitter account and a TweetChat.com account

How to Do It

1. Choose a time, date, and topic for the chat. This time should be sensitive to time zones and the topic should be mission related. Scheduling chats that occur regularly (e.g., weekly, monthly, quarterly) will help increase participation.
2. Determine what discussion format to use. Will there be a host from your organization who takes questions from Twitter on any topic or a set topic? Are there multiple hosts or is the chat free form, allowing anyone to respond at any time?
3. Create an account at www.tweetchat.com for your organization using its Twitter account.
4. Announce to Twitter, Facebook, and other appropriate channels when the chat will take place, what the topic will be, and other key details.
5. Kick off the chat with a tweet and Facebook update.
6. Use TweetChat to monitor the chat, responding when appropriate.
7. Thank participants for getting involved, publish a transcript of the chat, share lessons learned with the community, and announce the next event if possible.

A Closer Look   Hosting a scheduled chat on Twitter is similar to participating in other conversations involving hashtags, except that in this case your organization is leading the charge. Hosting a chat gives your nonprofit center stage and demonstrates its leadership, but also allows your supporters to get involved with your mission.

The key is to find a topic and format that makes sense for your type of nonprofit and audience. Here are a few ideas for different organization types:

- Higher Education—A chat could be held for alumni to discuss different aspects of the school, such as athletics, events, and campaigns.
- Arts and Cultural—Performing arts organizations, like theaters and ballets, can host chats featuring the stage performers that patrons will be seeing. A museum could host educational chats involving new or travelling exhibits.
- Environmental—Chats could be held around issues like climate change, deforestation, and water pollution.
- Animal Rights—A weekly chat could be set up featuring pets that are up for adoption—with the pets doing the tweeting! Sure, humans would be doing the actual typing, but creative ideas like this can draw attention.
- Human Rights—Hosting chats to discuss critical issues is something supporters would love to participate in, especially if actions and results are discussed.

Twitter chats also work well for organizing conversations with your nonprofits peers—staffers who have similar jobs or who work for similar organizations. Chats are regularly held around hashtags, like #NPTalk, #smNPchat, and #NPCons, which provide excellent information and networking for nonprofit professionals. Don't overlook these conversations, as they are great for connecting and engaging with key members of the community.

60 Organize a Tweetup

One of the greatest challenges nonprofit digital marketers face today is getting online supporters to take real-world action. A meet-up organized via Twitter, or a tweetup, is an effective way to provide your social supporters with an exclusive event they can attend.

For nonprofits with physical locations, volunteer spots, or accessible offices, a tweetup can be organized to bring supporters together and allow you to share your mission with them. A tweetup is a simple, quick, fun way to engage your Twitter audience in person, and hopefully convert some of them to donors, members, or volunteers.

What You Need   A Twitter account, a web site or Facebook page to post event information, and a physical location to hold an event

How to Do It
1. Plan a simple event that will bring supporters together for something (e.g., meeting, discussion, tour, networking, food and beverages).
2. Announce the event on Twitter and link to an event page. This can be a simple page on your web site with the tweetup information, or you can use Tweetvite.com, Facebook, or Eventbrite to organize the event.
3. Monitor Twitter for questions, feedback, and interest in the event.
4. Host the event. Be sure to hand out name tags and encourage attendees to write their Twitter handles on them.
5. Provide attendees a way to get more involved with your organization (e.g., newsletter subscriptions, volunteer opportunities, e-mail address).
6. Post updates and photos on your organization's Twitter account during the event.
7. After the event, thank the attendees and ask them if they want to do it again!
8. Measure the impact of the event based on what you were doing in step 5.

A Closer Look   To engage their online community, many nonprofits regularly hold tweetups. These simple events are easy to organize, low cost, and tap into existing programs that supporters are interested in. This gives organizations a great opportunity to bring online fans into the offline world.

Using tools like Tweetvite.com, a web service specifically designed to organize tweetups, supporters are notified on Twitter and other social channels about the upcoming event. This gets the word out to your social community without overwhelming the rest of your organization's audience. This exclusivity is part of the charm of tweetups.

Tweetups work really well for nonprofits that have physical locations, like theaters, public gardens, museums, and zoos. The Sacramento Zoo, Houston Zoo, and San Francisco Zoo have all held tweetups that lure online supporters with exclusive tours, behind the scenes access, and giveaways.

The American Museum of Natural History and the Museum of Science in Boston also hold tweetups onsite that offer many of the same things that the zoos do—access, socialization, and attention—things most supporters want. If your nonprofit does not have a great location, meet somewhere else like a park, library, bar, or school.

Engagement that offers something in return is always a smart move, and your supporters will remember that the next time they receive a fundraising pitch in the mailbox or inbox. Keep this in mind as you plan your next tweetup, and your supporters will be happy too!

 Reward Your Supporters for Checking In

Getting supporters to check in using foursquare is easier when you have something to offer them. When a user receives a special deal after checking in, their affinity toward your organization will increase along with the chance they'll talk about it with their friends. Reduced prices, membership deals, and special access are all things than can be worked into "Specials" on the foursquare platform. If you have supporters checking in already, taking it up a notch with these specials will make them feel, well, special!

What You Need A foursquare account and something to offer supporters

How to Do It A Mayor Special rewards the mayor, the person who has checked-in to a particular venue the most, with a coupon, discount, or other benefit. To create a Mayor Special on foursquare:

1. Create a foursquare account for your organization if you don't already have one.

2. Locate and claim your venue on foursquare (see Tactic 3). If your venue is not listed, add it to foursquare before you claim it.
3. Log in to foursquare and click "Manager Tools," then click "Campaigns."
4. Add a special by clicking "Start a Campaign" then "Add a Special."
5. Step 1 will ask you to determine what kind of special you want to run, and step 2 will ask you to decide when it happens.
6. Define the special by writing out how it will work in step 3. In the "Offer Description" field, write out what the offer is and how to claim it (e.g., Thanks to our Mayor for stopping by. Please grab a soft drink at the snack bar on us!)
7. Press the "Create Special" button.
8. Select the venue to use for the special, and press the "Select this Venue" button. In most cases, this will be your primary location.
9. Educate your staff on each special and how visitors should claim them.
10. Promote the specials through e-mail, social updates, door stickers, and other channels.

A Closer Look Checking into a venue is a fun social diversion, but if you've ever received something in return you know how exciting this simple act can be. Rewarding your supporters for checking in can increase visitors and reward their loyalty, so nonprofits with physical locations should jump at this opportunity to engage.

There are a few types of foursquare Specials to be created, and each can be customized with language and rewards. Friends and Swarm specials reward groups of people when they check in, the Newbie special is for first-time visitors, and the Check-In Special is given out every time someone checks in. The Mayor Special will reward the person who holds that title for the venue, and the Loyalty Special rewards visitors each time they check in. Finding the right special for your organization is key, and it's certainly okay to set up more than one to see what works.

The Vancouver Police Museum has set up a Mayor Special to reward their most loyal visitors. When the current foursquare mayor of the Museum checks in, he or she receives a 25 percent discount at the gift shop, plus free admission for them and a guest. This is a great deal that encourages the mayor to buy something in the gift shop and return in the future with a friend. https://foursquare .com/venue/114384

The Loyalty Special works well for enticing visitors to return over and over. The Taft Museum of Art in Cincinnati offers goodies to its loyal patrons that are unlocked every five check ins. The Mayor will get free admission every time he or she checks in. After five check ins, visitors will receive a free dessert, after 10 check ins, visitors will be rewarded with a free individual-level membership, and after 15 check ins a poster or illustrated guide is awarded. This is a great example of how to use foursquare to keep visitors engaged over a long period of time.

 ## Add Mission-Related Tips on foursquare

Like other social channels, foursquare has emerged as an effective platform for nonprofits looking to increase awareness and share information with supporters. The National Wildlife Federation has grown a large foursquare network that offers tips for its nature-loving followers, but even small nonprofits can make an impact with location-based services. Foursquare tips provide a simple point of interaction between you and the community. Providing useful tips is a great way to engage supporters on the go—and keep your organization, and its mission, top of mind.

What You Need   A foursquare account

How to Do It
1. Create a foursquare account for your organization.
2. Using the foursquare mobile application, check in to locations that relate to your mission.
3. Leave tips at these locations.
4. Promote your nonprofit's foursquare account to your supporters. If they follow you, the tips will be pushed to them as notifications.

A Closer Look If your nonprofit serves a local area, building a four-square presence can help deliver information to the community, advocate for causes, and connect supporters. The Charleston Parks Conservancy advocates for the increased usage and appreciation of local green spaces in the Charleston, South Carolina, community, so foursquare is a natural place to deliver mission-related information.

Tips are left at parks throughout Charleston, so foursquare users can learn more about the Conservancy's mission and connect via other channels. Executive Director Jim Martin says, "We exposed visitors to events and volunteer opportunities happening in those parks via tips. Wherever a foursquare user lists their Twitter handle, we follow them in the hopes they will follow us back."

While it is difficult to measure how effective tips are at getting attention, Jim adds, "It did raise awareness of the Conservancy and our work. Perhaps someone visits Cannon Park with their kids on a regular basis and notices the new garden. If they check in on four-square, they will associate that garden with us and hopefully consider volunteering to help maintain that garden or possibly make a donation to ensure its continued success."

When using emerging tools like foursquare, surprise results are around every corner and can often be beneficial. The Charleston Parks Conservancy found this out, as Jim shares, "foursquare has also proved to be a new way for us to find qualified volunteers and potential donors. If you check in to one of our parks, we can be pretty sure you have a vested interest in that park's success."

> Charleston Parks Conservancy's (www.charlestonparksconservancy.org) mission is to increase the quality, awareness, appreciation, and usage of Charleston's parks and green spaces.

 63   Create a Custom Badge on foursquare

There are many tools that foursquare offers corporations and nonprofits alike for raising awareness and engaging with their supporters, and custom badges are among the most coveted of these tools. A custom badge allows organizations to set badge-unlock rules that foursquare users have to follow to receive it. Although foursquare does not have an official program for nonprofits yet, it doesn't charge the select few nonprofits it works with to create custom badges. The company has created free badges for nonprofits including the Red Cross, the Guggenheim, and the New York Public Library to name a few.

What You Need   A highly visible event or unique campaign that will result in a high level of promotion for both your organization and foursquare, making this tactic more realistic for large or well-known organizations

How to Do It

1. The foursquare team needs at least a month of lead time to create a badge for most partners.
2. The business development team works closely with partners to develop badge-unlock rules and create a custom badge design.
3. Pitch your idea by filling out the form at https://foursquare .com/business/brands.

Exhibit 3.8   The New York Public Library's foursquare badge

Source: Courtesy of The New York Public Library (the name "The New York Public Library" and the lion logo are registered trademarks and the property of The New York Public Library, Astor, Lenox and Tilden Foundations and may not be used without the prior written consent of the Library); foursquare

A Closer Look   When The New York Public Library's (NYPL) landmark Stephen A. Schwarzman Building on Fifth Avenue and 42nd Street celebrated its Centennial in 2011, library-goers were invited to mark the occasion by checking in on foursquare. The Library partnered with foursquare to create a Find The Future Centennial Badge.

"We were especially excited about the partnership because the foursquare platform allows us to use the 90 virtual NYPL locations in the Bronx, Manhattan, and Staten Island as a canvas to promote physical visits and interaction with the Library in a fun way," says Johannes Neuer, NYPL eCommunications manager.

Foursquare users earned the red and yellow badge by checking in at NYPL locations. In addition to receiving the commemorative badge, participants were able to sign up for a complimentary one-year foursquare Friends Membership to the Library, including benefits such as exhibition previews, savings on event tickets, and discounts at The Library Shop. In addition, the Library offered specials such as monthly drawings for tickets to a LIVE from the NYPL event, a behind-the-scenes tour of the famed Lionel Pincus and Princess Firyal Map Division, and a photo op in front of the renowned Sue and Edgar Wachenheim III Trustees Room fireplace, immortalized in the movie *The Day After Tomorrow*.

"The NYPL's landmark building has been a New York institution for 100 years, and it's pretty amazing to see them starting their next 100 by embracing new ways to reach their fans," says Dennis Crowley, chief executive officer and co-founder of foursquare. "We hope the partnership will introduce even more people to all the Library has to offer."

> The mission of The New York Public Library (www.nypl.org) is to inspire lifelong learning, advance knowledge, and strengthen its communities.

 Participate in Giving Contests [with Caution]

There has been a lot of criticism about giving contests within the industry, primarily because of the community fatigue that they can cause. The thought is, a supporter taking an action is worth a lot—why waste the action on something that is not even core to your organization's mission? Many fundraising contests are geared toward votes. The average nonprofit does not have the marketing capacity or the e-mail list that the nonprofits that win often do. Before participating in a contest, be sure to consider if it makes sense for your organization, both from a timing and resource perspective.

What You Need   A 501(c)3 designation, a marketing list, and an established presence on social networks

How to Do It   Contests vary, but often rely on submitting an idea and or collecting votes or likes.

A Closer Look   As more and m   ore corporations are seeing the value of investing in social good programs versus throwing dollars into the black hole of advertising, there are an increasing number of contests that nonprofits are invited to participate in. How do you know what makes sense for your organization?

Geoff Livingston, author of *Welcome to the Fifth Estate*, wrote a very insightful post on Mashable[3] that provides some guidelines to consider before you participate in a contest. According to Geoff, it is a good idea to ask the following questions about your nonprofit organization:

- Do you have a realistic chance of being successful in the contest?
- Do you have the necessary time and resources to engage intensively in the contest to maximize the chances of winning?
- Will the campaign help build a new set of donors?
- Will participating in a contest strengthen capacity to integrate social media tools and networks into overall strategy?
- What kind of publicity will be generated from the application?
- Is there strong alignment between the contest's brand and your own?
- Does the contest align with your values, mission, and goals?
- Will participation add to or detract from potential donor fatigue?

---

[3]Geoff Livingston, "Are Social Media Giving Contests Good for Non-profits?", Mashable, June 11, 2010, http://mashable.com/2010/06/11/social-media-contests-non-profit.

- Can your organization give up and share control?
- If your nonprofit wins, can you implement any funding or other offering from the contest with your current infrastructure?
- If not, can your organization scale to meet the demands a winning opportunity brings?

 Launch a Social Contest on Facebook

Contests rule because they get people's attention, attract new supporters, and are fun for everyone involved—including your staff! A contest will spike engagement because of user-generated content, fan-voting, and social sharing components, and with the right prizes and theme, it can be closely aligned with your mission. Facebook is a great place to try a photo, video, essay, or write-in contest because each action is seen by a participant's network, amplifying the exposure to your cause.

What You Need   A Facebook page, a Twitter account, a web site, an account at Wildfireapp.com, and a budget to pay for the contest

How to Do It
1. Identify goals you want a contest to achieve, like attracting new Facebook fans, increasing web site referrals, and so on.
2. Design a contest theme that fits in with your mission and secure prizes. Having multiple prizes for first, second, and third places is a good idea.
3. Visit www.wildfireapp.com and create an account.
4. Follow the steps to create a promotion. Each contest type can be customized, so be sure to go through all the options.
5. Launch the contest on Facebook, your web site, and Twitter.
6. Once the contest has ended, solicit feedback from your supporters, collect metrics, and measure outcomes against goals.

A Closer Look   Whether it's a simple tweetaway on Twitter or a video response contest on YouTube (see Tactic 68), contests capture people's attentions and imaginations—making them perfect for nonprofits. Contests spread quickly because of the way Facebook's News Feed works, so they provide a great way to experiment and engage.

Companies like Wildfire (www.wildfireapp.com) help nonprofits launch social contests on Facebook, Twitter, and their web sites. The tool is very easy to use, so it really comes down to coming up with a great contest idea and a small budget to kick it off.

Once you have a great idea, make sure the contest is social in nature—that's how you'll get the biggest bang out of your online supporters. Here are some social components you want to make sure are included in your social contest:

- User-Submitted Content—Entering something into a contest will show up in a participant's news feed, alerting their friends to your campaign. Plus, participants are more likely to share the contest with their network when one of their own photos, videos, or essays is involved.
- Commenting—Make sure that supporters can comment on contest submissions, announcements, and news.
- Friend Invitations—Networks are made up of like-minded people, so encourage contest participants to invite their friends to play.
- Sharable Content—Add sharing capabilities to users' submissions, contest tabs, and other campaign-related materials.

 Build Stewardship Through Video

With an increasing demand from donors wanting to know how their gift was spent, stewardship is becoming even more important than it already was. A great way to share a gift's impact is through photos and video. If a donor cannot physically visit the construction site for the building they donated to, why not put a live feed of the progress on your homepage? With video, your organization can get very creative with keeping donors informed or simply say "thank you."

What You Need A video camera or webcam, a videographer, an editor, and a place to display the video (your web site, a DVD, or YouTube)

How to Do It
1. Determine the format of your video. Does it make sense to broadcast a livestream of a building being erected or will a pre-recorded video suffice?

2. Decide where you will display your video. YouTube is the most logical choice if you would like to expose your video to a larger audience. You may also consider pulling the YouTube video onto your web site.

3. Record and edit a short, compelling video that shows the impact of the donor's gift. This can even be personalized for major donors.

A Closer Look   OLPC is an MIT spin-off project that has designed the XO laptop to help children of the world learn, share, and create. The XO is rugged, for outdoor classrooms and harsh environments. It is ultra-low-power and can be charged by the sun. To date, 2.3 million laptops have been distributed in more than 40 countries such as Peru, Uruguay, Ethiopia, Rwanda, Afghanistan, Mongolia, and Haiti.

OLPC recorded a video thanking its supporters for making its work possible, but instead of a talking head, the organization turned to its recipients (see Exhibit 3.9). The "OLPC Thank You Video" has almost 20,000 views and in just over a minute, provides a view into this organization's great work (www.youtube.com/olpcfoundation).

The video starts with pictures from around the globe of children using the XO laptops. As the video progresses, a child shares how he uses his laptop to take pictures, do math, and draw. More children appear in the video, each from a different country, each saying thank you. The video provides a simple, yet powerful impact statement showing OLPC's supporters how their gifts are making a difference.

One Laptop Per Child (OLPC; www.laptop.org) is a nonprofit founded to improve education and eradicate poverty for children in developing nations.

  67   **Ask Supporters to Share Photos or Videos**

Asking supporters to share media is a great, easy way to get user-generated content on your page, making it more of a community. There is nothing more authentic than a first-hand account of how

Exhibit 3.9   One Laptop Per Child's YouTube channel

Source: One Laptop Per Child thank-you video rights are owned by OLPC Foundation; Courtesy of YouTube

your organization is affecting someone's life. As an added bonus, media sharing is a form of public engagement. Every time a supporter uploads a photo or video, it shows up in their stream so their own network will be exposed to your organization.

What You Need   A Facebook page

How to Do It
1. Be sure you have your page settings configured correctly by pressing "Edit Page" in the upper right-hand corner.
2. Under "Posting Ability" check "Users can add photos" and "Users can add videos."
3. In a status update, ask supporters to upload photos or video to your wall or tag your organization in a photo that demonstrates your mission in action.

A Closer Look   When Facebook rolled out some new features for photos in 2011, users started having the ability to tag a brand in a photo.

According to a *Fast Company* story[4] covering the new features, photo tags took "liking" a brand to the next level: "Now think about tags in photos. If you've tagged a photo in which you're wearing that cute pair of jeans, you don't simply like the idea of the designer. You've actually gone out and put down some of your hard-earned cash for their duds. Photo tags, then, become a much stronger signal of engagement. The downstream implications are many—and important." Rightly noted, when a user tags your organization in a photo, it becomes a part of your page, and your organization's story.

There are many ways to encourage submission of photos and videos. Here are a few ideas:

- Ask supporters to upload photos of their pets, their moms, their gardens—whatever your organization exists for.
- Hold a contest (see Tactic 65). Be sure to adhere to Facebook's promotion guidelines. Applications like Wildfire make it easy and painless to run a contest within the rules.
- Encourage supporters to share media (photos or videos) on the wall of your event.

 Hold a Video Response Contest

Video contests can be a great way to engage viewers on your YouTube channel and amass some user-generated content! You may even find a budding videographer whom you can ask to volunteer in the future. Uploading a picture is much easier than shooting and sharing a video, so be sure to give an incentive for your supporters to enter. The prize can be an experience—a chance to feed the sharks at your aquarium, or some (donated) video gear.

What You Need   A YouTube channel, a call to action, and a prize

How to Do It
1. The best way to launch a video response contest is with a video call to action! Keep it short and interesting.

---

[4]E. B. Boyd, "Why Facebook Photo Tags Are The New (And Possibly More Powerful) Likes," Fast Company, May 12, 2011, www.fastcompany.com/1752893/why-facebook-photo-tags-are-the-new-and-possibly-more-powerful-likes.

2. Include the terms and rules for your contest (be sure to abide by YouTube's contest rules). You may also want to clearly state that all levels of video are welcome, from amateur to professional.
3. Promote the prize to encourage participation.
4. Make sure that both comments and video responses are allowed in order to increase participation. You can set video responses to be approved right away or only after you review them, the latter being the safest choice.
5. Promote the contest and monitor participation.
6. Close the contest, announce the winners, and thank everyone for participating.

A Closer Look User-generated content is one of the most powerful aspects of social media, which is why video response contests can be so engaging. Michael Hoffman, CEO of See3 Communications, says, "With voting by the public and promotion by the content creators, these videos can get in front of a larger audience than an organization could achieve on its own."

It's that voting that helps get new supporters engaged. Michael adds, "Voting is a popular function online, a 'small ask' that is easy for many people to do, unlike making a donation, for example. Through voting, organizations can often introduce a large new potential group of supporters into an issue."

In 2009, YouTube partnered with Peace One Day to launch the "My Take on Peace" contest to commemorate the tenth anniversary of a Taliban ceasefire. The organization enlisted celebrity spokesperson Jude Law, who asked supporters to upload a video telling the world what they would do to create peace on September 21. The aim of the contest was for supporters to use the medium of film to tell the Peace One Day community what peace and Peace Day means to them.

The organization chose three finalists and turned to their supporters to vote for the winner. The winner, a school, was awarded with an HD video camera delivered by the founder of the organization. View the videos at www.youtube.com/peaceoneday on the playlist "My Take On Peace."

Another classic example of a nonprofit video response contest is The Humane Society of The United States' (HSUS) effort to stop animal fighting. In the wake of the Michael Vick dog-fighting scandal, the HSUS wanted to give supporters a way to express how they felt about this issue. HSUS enlisted wrestler Hulk Hogan to do a short video expressing his thoughts on animal fighting, with a call to action asking supporters to create their own videos and let the world know what they thought.

Carie Lewis, the director of emerging media at HSUS, says, "This was our first foray into user-generated content, and we had no idea what to expect. But, we were pleased with the results. Even though there were only 22 contest submissions, the voting portion of the contest brought in 2,000 new e-mail list members, 52,000 views of the Hulk Hogan PSA, and 90,000 views of the winning video." This level of engagement doesn't cost much, and goes a long way toward keeping supporters tuned into your mission.

 Create a Flickr Group to Support Your Mission

Photography is one of the best mediums a nonprofit has to share its mission with the world, and Flickr.com makes it easy to create a photo-based community with public groups. If your nonprofit has a visual appeal, creating a Flickr group is a great way to engage your supporters by allowing them to share their photos in a pool, start discussions, geo-tag content, and more. Giving your shutterbug supporters a place to share mission-based photos will keep them involved with your cause.

What You Need   A Flickr account, a Flickr group, and photos to add to this group

How to Do It
1. Sign-up for a Flickr account. Look at the Flickr for Good program before you get started (see Tactic 15).
2. Upload mission-related photos, and add titles, descriptions, and tags.
3. Access the "Groups" drop-down menu, and select "Create a New Group."
4. Choose the type of group you would like to use. Public groups that anyone can join are the best choice for this type of engagement.

5. Give the group a meaningful name and description.
6. Select the group safety level and press the "NEXT" button.
7. Decide if you would like the group's photos and discussions to be viewable to non-members, and press the "NEXT" button.
8. Customize the names of administrators, moderators, and members of the group, and press the "ALL DONE" button.
9. On the Administration page, there are many different settings you can update. Be sure to add any group rules, change the group's icon, create a Flickr web address for the group, and add some keywords to help people find it.
10. Begin promoting the group to your supporters via a campaign or program. Encourage them to upload images, leave comments, and start discussions. Hosting a contest is always a great way to get people involved (see Tactic 70).

A Closer Look   When you have a visual mission, using photos to engage supporters is an effective tactic. IMA understands this and uses Flickr to promote the 50,000 pieces in its collection and the 100 acres the building sits on. Jennifer Anderson, senior communications coordinator at the Museum, says, "When you're surrounded by nature's beauty, there is a lot that captures one's attention, which makes the IMA a favorite location for Indianapolis photographers, both amateur and professional. Flickr is an important way for us to share those images with other people, especially those who may not be able to physically visit our grounds."

IMA began its Flickr group as a way for visitors to share photos of the Museum, but also as a platform for patrons to communicate with each other. Jennifer says, "When Flickr came about, it seemed like a natural extension to our engagement goals—it was another way for our constituents to talk to us and to talk with each other."

Sharing is a great form of engagement for nonprofits, as it allows them to participate in an organization's mission in their own creative ways. Jennifer adds, "This goes back to the reason why people like to

The Indianapolis Museum of Art (IMA; www.imamuseum.org) serves the creative interests of its communities by fostering exploration of art, design, and the natural environment.

take pictures at the IMA—it's simply a beautiful place to be. It makes visitors feel good, and capturing that feeling in a snapshot is desirable. They want to share the image because they're proud of it."

Additionally, fans were encouraged to geo-tag photos taken throughout the Museum, especially out in the gardens. When uploaded to the Flickr group, this geographical data helps produce an interactive map of the property that displays visitor photos. All of this photo-related engagement can go a long way toward helping visitors create affinity and a sense of community around your nonprofit.

 Hold a Photo Contest

What's even more fun than sharing photos on social networking sites? Providing incentives that encourage your supporters to do so! Holding a photo contest is an easy way to engage supporters and build awareness of your cause. It can also be an effective tool in building excitement around a specific campaign or initiative. The benefits of hosting your contest on a social networking site versus your own web site include the collateral exposure you get and the ease of submission.

What You Need   A Flickr account, a call to action, and a prize

How to Do It
1. Ideally, launch the contest in support of a campaign or an issue you would like to raise awareness of (i.e., "Faces of Hunger").
2. Clearly state the terms and rules for your contest (be sure to abide by federal and state sweepstakes laws).
3. Set up a Flickr group for the contest and include clear instructions for how to tag or upload photos.
3. Promote the prize to encourage participation—whether it be bragging rights or a behind-the-scenes tour!

A Closer Look   The Civil War Trust holds an annual photo contest to capture images of the battlefields it seeks to preserve (see Exhibit 3.10). The 2011 contest had six categories that participants could enter photos in, including the Civil War 1861 category in honor of the Sesquicentennial, and even a high school-specific category.

The organization provided clear instructions on how to enter the contest, which was hosted on Flickr. It also took advantage

Exhibit 3.10   Civil War Trust's web page
Source: Courtesy of the Civil War Trust © 2011

The Civil War Trust (www.civilwar.org) is America's largest nonprofit organization devoted to the preservation of endangered Civil War battlefields. The Trust also promotes educational programs and heritage tourism initiatives to inform the public of the war's history and the fundamental conflicts that sparked it.

of Flickr's tagging abilities to manage entries into the different categories.

The organization awarded a variety of prizes, with the grand prize being a one-year membership and complimentary registration to an annual conference along with a plaque and recognition.

"The photo contest has gone on for 11 years, and in 2008, we began using Flickr to host it. At that point, interest in the contest exploded," says Jim Campi, Civil War Trust's policy and communications director. "Our American Civil War Battlefields photo group on Flickr makes it easy to upload photos on a 24/7 basis, allows everyone to see your photos, and it eliminates much of the administrative stress that our small organization would face otherwise. The contest also provides us with a wealth of images that enables a small organization such as ours to respond to media requests for images."

 ## Create a Photo Petition

Why send a signature when you can send a photo expressing your stance on an issue? Asking supporters to participate in a photo petition is a great way to engage them in your cause and send a clear message that not only has a name, but also a face. With the number of people with smartphones, photo sharing is easier than ever. Many organizations ask supporters to hold a sign that serves as the common thread between all of the photos. Get creative with this one!

What You Need   A campaign, a call to action, a platform for gathering and displaying photos, and an end recipient

How to Do It

1. Once you have identified a campaign that could benefit from petition support, identify who the end recipient of the petition will be.
2. Determine how you will gather and display the photos. This could be a custom-developed microsite or a Flickr Group (see Tactic 69).
3. Create a strong call to action. Do you want supporters to hold a sign showing their support of the issue, or will you take a more artistic route by asking people to take a picture in front of their favorite tree to fight over-development?

A Closer Look   Each year, Habitat for Humanity International celebrates World Habitat Day to raise awareness of the need for

Habitat for Humanity International (www.habitat.org) is a nonprofit, ecumenical Christian ministry that seeks to eliminate poverty housing and homelessness from the world and to make decent shelter a matter of conscience and action.

improved shelter. In support of the initiative, the organization collects photos to send to leaders in Washington, D.C. to persuade them that adequate housing for all should be a priority.

In 2010, Habitat built a photo wall on its web site on which supporters were asked to take a stand and post a photo answering the question "What would you build?" Participants wrote their answer on a piece of paper as a sign of support for the organization's work. They could then share their photo with friends and family by sending it as a message or by posting it on Facebook or Twitter. There was also a donate button built in for participants who wanted to contribute to the organization's work. Thousands of photos were gathered and sent to politicians to raise awareness of the housing issue

If you don't have a web developer in your budget, you can always take advantage of the free tools on Flickr, including Groups. Many organizations opt to host their petitions on Flickr because of its social nature.

 Organize a Petition on Twitter

Since many politicians have taken to Twitter to spread their messages, why not direct your advocacy efforts toward reaching them there? There are many services that help you create a petition and tweet it out to followers so others can "sign" (tweet) the petition. Act.ly, in particular, displays the number of tweets and identifies recent signers. Users can choose to direct a petition at a specific Twitter account and track how long it takes for the owner of that account to respond. Talk about the hot seat!

What You Need   A Twitter account with some followers, a target account, and an issue to advocate

How to Do It
1. Visit www.act.ly.com and sign in with your Twitter credentials.
2. Enter the account that you want to target and the subject of the petition and press "Create."
3. Enter additional text for the petition and save petition.
4. Press "Sign and Tweet" and your petition will go live.
5. Make it go viral by embedding a tweet button or posting the petition on a variety of social networks.

A Closer Look   Greenpeace used Act.ly to petition @Microsoft to "cut its emissions and speak up for a planet-saving climate deal in Copenhagen." The petition (http://act.ly/1h3) called for Microsoft to commit to cut its own absolute carbon emissions and use its money and influence to support strong international and U.S. climate legislation. The petition also included a spoof video poking fun at Microsoft executives and accused the company of funding anti-climate lobbying.

With 268 tweets reaching 143,988 users, the petition had a lot of support. Microsoft tweeted a response, sharing a link to a statement on what the company is doing to support COP15 and reduce environmental impact and decided to send executives to the Copenhagen climate summit. Greenpeace responded with a post of its own, breaking down different things it thought Microsoft should be doing and thanking its Twitter followers for taking action.

The vast majority of petitions on Act.ly (many of which are directed at @whitehouse and @StateDept) are not responded to, but are effective at raising awareness of an issue.

> Greenpeace (www.greenpeace.org) is an independent global campaigning organization acting to change attitudes and behavior, to protect the environment, and promote peace.

 ### 73   Socialize Your Internal Communications

Is your intranet tired? Does no one read the monthly newsletter that you so laboriously concoct? Spice things up with some real-time social sharing! Whether it be a private social network (see Tactic 77), or an internal blog or microblog, make it fun and more people will participate. Often, nonprofit professionals wear many hats, so an internal social network provides the perfect way for the small shop, or the largest of organizations to crowdsource ideas, answer questions, and share successes in a non-traditional format.

What You Need   Depending on the type of channel you choose, you can use a restricted Wordpress installation, a private Facebook group, a more sophisticated online community platform, or a free service like Yammer, which we will use for this example. Yammer is an internal microblogging service that provides a free way for users to communicate, collaborate, and share more easily and efficiently.

How to Do It

1. Visit Yammer.com and sign up by entering your work e-mail address. *Only those with an official @yournonprofit.org e-mail address can join.*
2. Validate your account by following the instructions sent to your e-mail address.
3. Complete your profile and add your photo.
4. Invite other people to join. *This is key—even though you will see that membership spreads like wildfire once people catch wind of it.*
5. Follow people. If you are at a large organization, this is extremely useful. If you are at a small organization, you may wish to view the "company feed."
6. Employees at large organizations may wish to create groups, which are subsets of the network, to make it easier to segment conversations based on teams.
7. Be sure to check out Yammer's desktop and mobile apps to make it easier to access the network.

A Closer Look   With a staff of more than 20 people in Washington, D.C. and additional remote workers across the country, it was often difficult for individuals at The National Society of Collegiate Scholars to stay connected with each other's work.

According to Mishri Someshwar, NSCS's director of marketing and public relations, one of the biggest challenges that organizations like NSCS face is building a culture and a process by which employees can share and become aware of each others' achievements, as well as appreciate the value that their colleagues bring. "This can be challenging in large organizations where staff are

The National Society of Collegiate Scholars (NSCS; www.nscs.org) is a nonprofit honor society for high-achieving first- and second-year college students.

scattered across the globe and functional groups," says Mishri. "It can be equally challenging for small organizations where staff are stretched to the limit with a variety of tasks and duties."

The organization started using Yammer in January 2009. What started as an easy way to share mass messages about goodies in the break room quickly evolved to become a way to share more important news and share successes.[5]

With Yammer, NSCS has been able to improve collaboration, reduce e-mail clutter, improve insight, and strengthen team culture.

 ## 74   Treat Your Social Networks Like V.I.P.s

Each and every one of your social network followers/subscribers/ likers have something in common, no matter what platform they engage with you on. They are interested in what you have to say. So much so that they subscribe to an ongoing stream of information about your organization and its cause. That is pretty special in a day when the average open rate for nonprofit e-mail is 13 percent.[6] Your mom always told you to say thank you, but this deserves something more. Roll out the red carpet for your fans—they deserve it!

What You Need   An inventory of all of your social networks, breaking news, giveaways, and/or premium benefits

How to Do It
1. Identify the networks you want to focus on—Facebook and Twitter are a good start.
2. Determine the frequency and/or nature of your offer.
3. Decide what makes sense for your audience and your organi- zation. What would your supporters value most?

A Closer Look   The best kind of reward is one that is least expected. Simple giveaways on your social networks or exclusive deals are great ways to make your supporters feel appreciated. In addition to holding

[5]Mishri Someshwar, "DC Nonprofit Use Yammer To Build Culture, Reduce Clutter," Yammer, March 14, 2011, http://blog.yammer.com/blog/2011/03/ mishri-someshwar-yammer-nscs.html.
[6]2011 eNonprofit Benchmarks Study, www.e-benchmarksstudy.com.

contests (see Tactics 65, 68, and 70 for ideas) to engage supporters, or encouraging check-ins with loyalty specials (see Tactic 61),
you can also give away random prizes to supporters (i.e., your 500th
Facebook fan or 1000th Twitter follower, or the person who commented on your blog the most in a month) without telling them up
front as a way to say "thanks."

The best thing is, it doesn't have to be something expensive.
Does your organization have a store with logo wear? Can you offer
up some free tickets to an event or production? Upgraded membership? These types of items are great gifts.

If you don't have the budget or items that would work for a
giveaway, you may want to consider reaching out to some of your
sponsors for in-kind donations. Most businesses are more than willing
to donate goods in exchange for a little publicity. Deals are another
inexpensive way to reward supporters. "The first 25 Twitter followers
that stop in today get $5 off admission!"

You can also look at giveaways that don't cost anything—premium
benefits like a meet and greet with the cast of a production or a
behind-the-scenes look at the shark tank. Experiences are priceless!

Another free way to say thanks is by filling your social networks
in on big news first. Real-time communication is a huge benefit of
social media. If your organization has a big announcement about a
new exhibit or breaking news about a medical breakthrough, share
it with your followers first!

 ## Create Your Own Online Community

This tactic may not make sense for every organization, but for many,
creating their own online community or "house social network," provides many benefits, including access to data, and more control over
functionality, branding, and privacy. House social networks provide a
unique place where constituents can interact with one another and
the organization around a very specific cause or interest. According
to the 2011 Nonprofit Social Network Benchmark Report, nearly
all nonprofits have a presence on commercial social networks
(especially Facebook) while just 13 percent have a house network.
While networks like Facebook are primarily used for marketing,
house networks are more commonly used for program delivery.

What You Need   A platform, a project budget, and a community manager

How to Do It

1. Begin by creating objectives, a staffing plan, and a budget for the project.
2. Define the technical aspects; that is, integration to other systems.
3. Determine what programs you will support in the community.
4. Research platforms and associated costs.
5. Work with the vendor or a consultant to configure the community.
6. Create a deployment strategy that makes the most of the launch and supports ongoing recruitment of new members.
7. Continually nurture and build the community by addressing members' needs and incorporating feedback, while building the depth of the community's offerings.

Exhibit 3.11   Christopher & Dana Reeve Foundation's Paralysis Community home page

Source: Courtesy of the Christopher & Dana Reeve Foundation

A Closer Look   In an effort to expand its reach and to become the go-to resource for information on care and cure of spinal cord injury, the Christopher & Dana Reeve Foundation turned to social media. The organization was successful in building community on Facebook and Twitter, but did not have a lot of control over the data. In an effort to harness that information and better connect its constituents, the Foundation decided to implement a house social network on Blackbaud Social technology (see Exhibit 3.11). The Paralysis Community now provides a place where people living with and caring for others with paralysis can interact in a private, secure environment.

"In less than a month, 600 people signed up and since then, that growth has continued," says Rob Gerth, Christopher & Dana Reeve Foundation's director of digital media. "An important piece of having our own private community is to collect the data and use that data to serve our community members better—that's what it's all about for us."

The Christopher & Dana Reeve Foundation (www.christopherreeve.org) is dedicated to curing spinal cord injury by funding innovative research, and improving the quality of life for people living with paralysis through grants, information, and advocacy.

Fundraise

There is a great debate on whether or not social media can be effective for fundraising. And although fundraising should not be the primary goal of your social media program, it can be a rewarding component of it. This chapter will feature many examples where innovative nonprofits have leveraged Facebook, Twitter, YouTube, and other platforms to raise some serious funds for some great causes.

According to the 2011 Nonprofit Social Network Benchmark Report,[1] Facebook is the most popular commercial social network for fundraising, with half of nonprofits responding that they used Facebook to raise money from individual donors. Of those actively raising money on Facebook, 35 percent have raised less than $1,000, and less than 1 percent of nonprofits have raised more than $100,000 via Facebook in the 12-month reporting period. The report concluded that if an organization dedicates the budget and staff to the task, even a small charity can raise $100,000 or more on Facebook. Take that naysayers!

So where do you start? At the very least, it is a good idea to incorporate ways to give on your social networks or alternately, a link to your donation site. It may make sense for you to run a social media-specific fundraising campaign, and it definitely makes sense to augment your existing fundraising campaigns with calls to action on your social networks. Social media should not be approached as

---

[1]"2011 Nonprofit Social Network Report," http://nonprofitsocialnetworksurvey.com/files/2011%20NPO%20SN%20Benchmark%20Report%20Final.pdf.

a separate channel, but as a toolset to augment your existing online campaigns. Take a look at your web site analytics—odds are that social media platforms are among the top referring sites if you are active in these channels.

The added benefit of social-media platforms is the viral nature of them. If a supporter retweets, likes, or shares your appeal, the appeal is now reaching an entirely new set of potential supporters. That kind of exposure is ideal for a cause-marketing partnership, allowing your organization to partner with brands that would like to be associated with your cause.

Fundraising via social media has to be approached authentically, with respect for your communities, and in a unique way. Some of the most successful campaigns started off with a simple idea focused on awareness with the added benefit of fundraising. Others leverage powerful tools and techniques like Facebook Causes, peer fundraising, and location-based platforms to engage supporters in the fundraising process. Experiment and ultimately invest in what is one of the most promising growth areas for fundraising.

 ## Raise Money with Causes

Causes was one of the first social fundraising tools to hit the market, and continues to be an effective and easy-to-use method for raising money through your Facebook network. Creating a Cause on Facebook will provide an easy way for Facebook users to give to your organization, advocate for your mission, and spread the word to their own networks. Many Facebook users look for a Causes tab when they visit nonprofit pages, so be sure to have yours set up and ready to accept donations.

What You Need   A Facebook page, and an account at Cause's Nonprofit Partner Center

How to Do It

1. Create an account and sign in to Cause's Nonprofit Partner Center at https://nonprofits.causes.com.

2. Start a cause by visiting www.causes.com/causes/new. Be sure to brand your page well by including photos, video, and mission-related stories.

3. Link your personal profile to your nonprofit account by logging in to the Nonprofit Partner Center and visiting this page: http://nonprofits.causes.com/account/facebook_ accounts.

4. Create a fundraising project or petition-based campaign for your supporters.

5. Add Causes as a tab on your organization's Facebook page by visiting www.facebook.com/causes. Click the "Add to My Page" link, select your organization's page, press the "Get Started" button, and follow the steps. Remember that you can change the name of this tab from "Causes" to something like "Donate."

6. Promote you causes via your social networks, e-mail list, web site, and newsletters.

A Closer Look Depending on who you ask, Causes will be described as either the best way to raise money on Facebook or a red herring. Regardless, raising ANY money is a positive, so ignoring Causes is not a great strategy if you're looking to turn social media fans into actual donors.

Setting up Causes as a Facebook tab is pretty simple, so once that is complete you'll need to find the best way to use the tool for your audience. Here are a couple of nonprofits who have seen good results using Causes:

The Nature Conservancy has raised more than $400,000 using Causes, and continues to prominently feature the application on its Facebook page as a "Donate" tab—it's the first tab under Wall and Info. The organization uses buttons to make it easy to donate and join, and also features quotes from actual donors in a "Why I Give" section. The page continues by featuring other ways to give, prompting supporters to create a birthday wish (see Tactic 77), donate by text, or set up a recurring gift.

Project Night Night is a small nonprofit that has made a big impact with its Causes tab. Featuring a photo viewer and desired campaign outcome prominently, its Causes tab communicates its mission well. The tab also features a love "thermometer" showing total donations and the campaign goal, information on how donations will be used, and buttons prompting supporters to donate and share the cause.

 ## Encourage Supporters to Make a Wish

Alternative giving, or donating in honor of someone instead of purchasing physical gifts, is a great way to show support of an organization while giving a gift with meaning. By providing your supporters with the information and tools to easily reach out to their social networks, they can create a wish dedicated to your organization, raising funds and awareness. Causes' Wish feature helps users donate their birthday, their wedding, their run, and so on to charity, or you can choose to build the functionality into your site with peer fundraising tools.

What You Need   A Causes account and an awareness campaign geared at informing supporters about the tool

How to Do It
1. Sign up your organization for a Causes account at Causes.com.
2. Add instructions for creating a wish under your organization's "Ways to Give" section and follow the tips below.

A Closer Look   Causes' Wish feature is the easiest way to encourage alternative giving and is so intuitive that it practically does the fundraising for you. More than $12 million has been raised with the Wish feature for various causes.[2] Supporters start off at http://wishes .causes.com and follow the steps to create a wish.

Causes offers the following tips for nonprofits and cause administrators[3]:

1. Add a Wish widget to your web site.
2. Send a bulletin to your cause members asking them to make a Wish for your cause.
3. Send an e-mail to your e-mail list asking your supporters to create a Wish for you.

---

[2]"Create A Causes Wish," http://wishes.causes.com/.
[3]"Create A Causes Wish," http://wishes.causes.com/.

4. Make sure your board members, employees, interns, and supporters know about this opportunity.

5. Use your web site, Twitter feed, newsletter, e-newsletter, put it in e-mail signatures, or use other ways you talk to your existing supporters to get the word out.

6. Get creative—start a contest for who can raise the most money for their birthday next month.

The American Cancer Society took this concept in house, declaring itself "the official sponsor of birthdays" and built a site at http://morebirthdays.com where users could create their own birthday fundraising pages and participate in a variety of interactive birthday-themed features.

 ## Create a Facebook Donation Tab

This tactic uses the same technology and process for creating a tab as tactics 46 and 47 do, but focuses on fundraising. A generic donation tab should be automatic on your Facebook page. The content can easily be swapped out for seasonal campaigns throughout the year. Although we don't recommend you make this the default page for new fans, it should be placed high up in the order so potential supporters can easily find it.

What You Need A Facebook page, a web server, a web developer, and a donation form

How to Do It
1. Refer to Tactic 47 for setting up a custom tab.
2. When designing the webpage, incorporate the donation form of your choice.

A Closer Look The Planned Parenthood Action Fund Facebook page (facebook.com/plannedparenthood) makes use of several custom tabs. The Donate tab is positioned in the highest spot available, making it extremely easy for visitors to the page to find it.

When visitors land on the tab, they are immediately thanked for supporting Planned Parenthood Federation of America with a tax-deductible donation. (Wait, did I make one? Guess I have

The Planned Parenthood Action Fund (www.plannedparenthoodaction.org) is the advocacy and political arm of Planned Parenthood Federation of America. The organization works in the streets, in the states, and in Washington, DC, to advance women's reproductive health and rights.

to now!) The organization does a great job of reminding donors what their money is going to support: "Your support will help us continue to protect and promote women's health in the halls of Congress and in communities across the country. It will make a world of difference for the millions of women, men, and teens who rely on local Planned Parenthood health centers every day."[4]

Even though it is the same form essentially, the organization does give donors the option to make the gift directly on the Planned Parenthood web site before presenting the form. The next thing Planned Parenthood gets right is the fact that their form has ask amounts. They could have just thrown a donation button up there, but instead, they have suggested increments of $15 to $500. Following the donation form, there is a default opt in to future communications from Planned Parenthood.

 ## 79   Hold a Tweetathon

A tweetathon borrows in concept from the traditional fundraising telethon, but takes place on Twitter. The online event usually benefits one charity and takes place over a set period of time. Some tweetathons enlist celebrities to help spread the word, while some offer prizes. Others focus on raising the number of followers for an organization's Twitter account and accept pledges for every 100 new followers within the time period. Like many social media fundraising tactics, the key is to be original—there are no steadfast rules!

What You Need   A Twitter account with a high number of followers, or a group of people willing to tweet on your behalf, and a way to accept donations

---

[4]Planned Parenthood Facebook page, www.facebook.com/plannedparenthood.

How to Do It

1. Determine when and how long you will hold the tweetathon. It is a good idea to set a short time period (less than a day) to create a sense of urgency.

2. Develop your call to action. Is your goal to raise money and increase the number of followers for your organization? Set a specific ask amount and tie it to the goal. Have your Twitter helpers reference your organization's handle in every tweet. Be sure to promote your Twitter account on the donation page.

3. Make the event your own. Offer a twibbon for those who have donated (see Tactic 52). Make it a contest by "rewarding" the donor who puts you over your goal with a behind-the-scenes tour of your organization or with a donated prize.

A Closer Look   Scott Stratten, organizer of the multiple tweetathons that have raised upward of $50,000 shared nine key areas that led to their success on his blog Unmarketing[5]:

1. Organizer span of influence—In order to be successful with a tweetathon, you need to have pre-existing networks of supporters, or influencers who can help. As Scott points out, you can't just open an account on Twitter and start asking for donations. Twitter is a community and a conversation, not a pitch platform.

2. The cause—Choose a cause or program that everyone can relate to, not just a select few.

3. The raffle—The tweetathons provided an entry into a prize raffle for each donation. Most of the raffle prizes were donated by people Scott had previously connected with on Twitter.

4. The set donation suggestion—There were two suggested donation levels set for the tweetathons. The first was $12 and included one entry into a raffle, the second level was $120 and got donors 10 entries, and a complementary web site review from Scott, an accomplished author and consultant.

5. The short timeframe—12-hour events created a sense of excitement and urgency.

---

[5]Danny Brown, "How to Raise Money on Twitter-Tweetathon 101," July 22, 2009, http://www.unmarketing.com/2009/07/22/how-to-raise-money-on-twitter-tweetathon-101.

6. The number of tweets—Scott tweeted almost every minute, driving people back to the donation page.
7. The social proof retweet—Scott retweeted donation tweets, which increased exposure and led the campaign to become a trending topic.
8. Cause soldiers—Scott refers to the tweetathon supporters as a "Tweeting Army" and notes that they added momentum to the campaign.
9. Focus—The only call to action for the tweetathon was to donate.

 Launch a Sponsored Tweet Campaign

Like many of the other fundraising initiatives on social media, a sponsored tweet campaign involves a cause-marketing partnership or a major donor. A sponsor funds a challenge gift and then it is up to the organization and its supporters to meet the challenge. In this case, supporters simply retweet a message, spreading awareness among their networks and optionally contributing to the donation through their action.

What You Need   A cause-marketing partner or major donor, a campaign, and a way to track retweets

How to Do It
1. Secure a partner that will fund the campaign and establish a challenge gift amount.
2. Determine how much each retweet will be worth. (Somewhere between $1 and $10 is an ideal amount.)
3. Create a concise message focused on awareness with a link to donate.
4. Ask your supporters to retweet your message.
5. Record how many people retweeted your message and claim your donation.

A Closer Look   In 2010, Malaria No More raised the bar for a standard sponsored tweet campaign and partnered with the Case Foundation, Twitter, Twitpay, Katalyst Media, and the UN Special Envoy for Malaria's "Social Media Envoys" to raise direct donations through retweets.

Launched by Malaria No More to raise awareness and funds and in recognition of World Malaria Day, the campaign raised

Malaria No More (www.malarianomore.org) leverages high-impact awareness campaigns to engage the world, global advocacy to rally leadership, and strategic investments in Africa to accelerate progress, build capacity, and save lives.

funds for 89,000 mosquito nets[6] and created mass awareness of the Malaria epidemic.

Here's how it worked:

@MalariaNoMore asked supporters to retweet the following message:

RT: Malaria kills a child every 30 secs. Nets #endmalaria. So do RTs. RT2Give $10 http://rt2give.com/t/425.

Once supporters retweeted the message, if they were RT2Give users, they received a direct message asking for a confirmation of their donation. For new users, Twitpay automatically sent an @reply message with instructions on how to join.

The Case Foundation matched each $10 up to $25,000 made through Twitpay and through the organization's text-to-give program that ran concurrently. The campaign resulted in 178,000 tweets and more than 55 million media impressions.

 Organize a Fundraising Campaign through Twitter

Twitter is an amazing platform for connecting with other like-minded people in real time. That is why, when it comes to fundraising, it is a great tool for organizing and marketing a campaign. Whether the campaign incorporates real "in-person" events or the activity all takes place in a virtual setting, Twitter can help your campaign travel and multiply. Plus, since Twitter is free and attracts a very distinct demographic, you get the added benefit of running an efficient campaign and reaching supporters you may not otherwise reach.

What You Need A Twitter account, a great idea, and a plan for accepting monetary and/or in-kind donations

---

[6]Erica Lichtenberger, "Twitterers & Texters Double Down to Fight Malaria," Buzzwords blog, April 23, 2010, www.malarianomore.org/news/blog/twitterers-texters-double-down-fight-malaria.

How to Do It   This tactic does not have cut and dried steps, rather it takes some ingenuity. Read the examples below for inspiration and get creative! If you are raising funds for the first time, there are many free or low-cost donation tools available. Many of these campaigns rely on sponsors or cause-marketing partners to take them to the next level.

A Closer Look   Here are three unique examples to get your creative juices flowing:

1. Twestival (www.twestival.com)

At the top of the pack of Twitter fundraising campaigns is Twestival. This Twitter-Festival that is organized with and promoted on Twitter takes place in cities all over the world on a single day to raise money for a selected cause, such as clean water and education, or in Twestival Local's case, to raise money for local causes (see Exhibit 4.1). Each city's fundraising event is unique, yet is guided by the Twestival vision. Since 2009, more than 200 cities have participated in Twestival raising nearly $1.75 million. (And who said you can't raise money via social media?)

Amanda Rose, organizer of Twestival says: "The first Twestival was actually a single event that happened in London in September 2008. We organized it under short timescales, bringing the local Twitter community offline for a night to connect and support a local homeless shelter. It was a sold-out event and after that finished, I started thinking about all of the other amazing communities that are being created around the world thanks to Twitter. I knew if I found the right cause to support, I could use social media to mobilize my global network to join me in something powerful on one day."

2. Holiday Tweet Drive (www.tweetdrive.org)

A dream of Philadelphia student/entrepreneur Harrison Kratz, the first Holiday Tweet Drive was held in October 2010 to leverage the power of social media to collect toys for children during the holiday season. Much like Twestival, the 2010 Holiday Tweet Drive consisted of organizing via Twitter and convening at real-world events. Twenty-five individual tweetups were held and 2000 toys were collected and donated to local charities. A Tweet Drive was also held in March 2011 following the natural disasters in Japan.

Exhibit 4.1   Twestival home page
Source: Courtesy of Connect the Dots Foundation

3. Epic Thanks (www.epicthanks.org)

Another brilliantly successful campaign from the folks at Epic Change, Epic Thanks (formerly Tweetsgiving) is an example of a virtual fundraising event. A global celebration that seeks to change the world through the power of gratitude, supporters are encouraged to express their gratitude through thank you cards and tweets, and are given the option to make a donation to support Epic Change's work in supporting change-makers around the world. (Nearly $14,000 was raised from 179 individuals in 2010.) The interactive site includes social plugins pulling in activity from multiple social networks.

Increase Conversions with Video Overlays

YouTube is an effective channel for sharing your organization's mission with supporters, but the ultimate goal of a social media program should be to get people to take action. YouTube's video overlays help do this by displaying appeals directly in videos which can be linked to donation forms, newsletter subscription pages, or volunteer information. If your video is compelling, it should drive a desire for supporters to act—video overlays will help them take that first step, and hopefully make a donation.

What You Need   A YouTube account for your organization, a video, and a donation page on your web site

How to Do It
1. Apply for YouTube's Nonprofit Program by visiting http://www.youtube.com/nonprofits, and pressing the "Apply" button.
2. Access your YouTube account and click "Uploaded Videos" under "My Videos."
3. Find the video you would like to add an overlay to, and click "Edit."
4. Locate the "Call-to-Action Overlay" section and fill in all the required fields. Make sure your language is clear and concise, and that the page you are linking to makes it clear how visitors take action.
5. Press the "Save Changes" video.
6. Watch your video on YouTube to see that the overlay and link are working properly.

A Closer Look   YouTube video overlays work just like other similar advertisements on YouTube—they display in the bottom of the video and link to an external page. These overlays do not hide the video and can be minimized by the viewer at any time. This makes them a great way to include an "ask" without being too intrusive.

Think about a clear and concise call to action, similar to the text you would include in a Google AdWords ad. Driving viewers to a donation pages is ideal, so the copy you use is critical. You do not have many characters to play with, so think about how you can get your message across in only a few words.

A great example of successful fundraising using video overlays involves charity: water, which included one on its World Water Day video (see Exhibit 4.2). charity: water's call to action was clear and concise. It read, "Give a person clean water. 100% of your gift directly funds water wells." This was followed by a link to

Exhibit 4.2   charity: water YouTube video page

Source: Courtesy of charity: water; YouTube

www.charitywater.org/donate, where the viewer was taken once they clicked the overlay.[7]

When the video was featured on YouTube's homepage in support of World Water Day, charity: water raised more than $10,000 in 24 hours. While the exposure to YouTube's audience certainly helped contribute to these phenomenal results, the simplicity of the overlay itself and the nature of the campaign can easily be duplicated by nonprofits of any size. So if you have a great video that is being watched, but sure to add an overlay and drive some viewers to take action.

Use Video Annotations as Calls to Action

Including calls to action in marketing materials is a critical step for any organization focused on converting viewers into donors, volunteers, or advocates. Annotations are clickable objects embedded in videos,

---

[7]Ramya Raghavan, "YouTube Nonprofit Raises $10,000 in One Day Using Overlay Ads," Broadcasting Ourselves blog, March 27, 2009, http://youtube-global .blogspot.com/2009/03/youtube-nonprofit-raises-10000-in-one.html.

and YouTube's Nonprofit Program allows organizations to link these to donation, subscription, and volunteer pages on their web sites. Annotations are easy to set up and turn your videos into interactive multimedia pieces that help supporters take action.

What You Need   A YouTube account for your organization, a video, and a donation, subscription, or volunteer page on your web site

How to Do It
1. Apply for YouTube's Nonprofit Program by visiting http://www.youtube.com/nonprofits, and pressing the "Apply" button.
2. Access your YouTube account and click "Uploaded Videos" under "My Videos."
3. Find the video you would like to add an overlay to, and click "Edit."
4. Access the "Annotations" tab.
5. Determine where you want the call to action to appear in the video, press the "Add Annotation" button, and select the type of annotation you want to use.
6. Add a link pointing to a donation page, then press the "Save" and "Publish" buttons.
7. Test the annotation to make sure it is working properly.

A Closer Look   YouTube's Nonprofit Program really takes care of organizations trying to make a difference, and that's why they've made an extended feature set available through the program. The ability to link to external pages is something account holders can only do through the Nonprofit Program, so be sure to take advantage of this powerful functionality.

If you've made a compelling video that will attract a lot of attention (see Tactic 41), using annotations to embed calls to action will help convert your social media effort into real results. These annotations can be added at the beginning of the video, at the end, or creatively placed throughout—the options are almost endless.

Choosing the right call to action is important if you want to be sure the activity is tied to your organizational goals. You may be trying to raise money, increase subscriptions, or attract volunteers—so your calls to action should reflect this. Choose wisely, as this may be your only chance to grab a viewer's attention.

StillerStrong.org takes an effective approach toward video annotations by persistently including them throughout each video. During

Exhibit 4.3   StillerStrong YouTube video page

Source: Courtesy of LIVESTRONG and Alpheus Media; YouTube

video production, a graphic is placed at the bottom of each video featuring four calls to action. Invisible YouTube annotations are used to turn these into buttons, which can be clicked at anytime throughout the video (see Exhibit 4.3). Along with social sharing links for Twitter and Facebook, as well as a link to its web site, StillerStrong includes a "Donate Online" link pointing directly to a form on its web site.

So, get creative with annotations, and you'll find that your videos really can entice supporters to make a donation. Providing this opportunity directly in the video, rather than using a typical URL-based call to action at the end of the video, will reduce barriers and increase conversions.

Enable Social Giving with Peer Fundraising Tools

The old fundraising adage rings true with social media as well. People give to people. Peer fundraising web sites provide nonprofits with a platform to share fundraising tools with their supporters so they can reach out to their personal networks for donations. In the fundraising toolbox, many solutions have built-in social media integration, easily allowing for fundraisers to extend their fundraising ask to their Twitter and Facebook networks as well. While these systems range widely in cost and complexity, fees are usually transaction based, making the software accessible for non-profits of all sizes.

What You Need   A peer fundraising platform, a fundraising campaign or event, and a training plan for your volunteer fundraisers

How to Do It
1. Do your research. There are a ton of options to choose from. A good place to start is from a donor point of view—what causes have you given to through peer fundraising software? What was your experience like with them?
2. Ask for recommendations. Reach out to your peer organizations to see what they are using.
3. Research the level of the solution's social-media integration and ask about future roadmap plans.
4. Opt for a vendor that will provide great support along the way and has a track record of success.
5. Once the system is in place, be sure to provide volunteer fundraisers with the training they need to make the most of it through videos, tip sheets, reminder e-mails, and so on.

A Closer Look Event participants using peer fundraising software are especially successful when incorporating social networks into their ask arsenal. According to a study[8] by Blackbaud and Charity Dynamics, event participants who adopted integrated social media tools in addition to basic online fundraising increased their fundraising by as much as 40 percent compared to their peers who didn't.

"The popularity of social media web sites like Facebook, Twitter, and YouTube has given rise to promising new ways for event participants to raise money online," says Mark Davis, co-author of the study "Making Event Participants More Successful with Social

---

[8]Donna Wilkins and Mark C. Davis, "Making Event Participants More Successful with Social Media Tools," blackbaud, June 2011, http://www.blackbaud.com/files/resources/downloads/WhitePaper_Event ParticipantsSocialMedia.pdf.

Media Tools" and Blackbaud's director of enterprise Internet solutions. "While some people still doubt the fundraising potential of these tools, special event participants continue to be an exception and have shown strong fundraising success by tapping into the power of social networking."

Additional findings of the study include:

- Event participants who used Twitter raised more money and reached more donors than non-Twitter users, tripled their personal fundraising goals, and raised nearly 10 times more online.
- Fundraising via Facebook has evolved in both process and success from user initiated to organization prompted to sophisticated Facebook applications that automate status updates by prompting participants throughout event campaigns.
- YouTube users performed the strongest offline when compared to participants who were using other social media tools and are more likely to balance their use of both online and offline channels to tell their stories and conduct fundraising activities.
- Donors attracted through social media are more likely new to an organization. On average, 75 percent of donors through social media are new to organizations versus an average of 50 percent of all donors in support of participants.

So, not only will your event fundraisers be more successful by using integrated social media tools, they will be more likely to attract new supporters to the organization.

 ## 85   Launch a Check In for Charity Campaign

What if your supporters could check in and earn more than a virtual badge? With a well-designed check in for charity campaign, they can earn a donation for your organization! Check in for charity campaigns typically are supported through a cause-marketing partnership pairing a corporate donor with a nonprofit. They are sometimes funded by a major donor. They are run using a location-based application like foursquare or Gowalla. They result in a donation for every check in and are usually funded up to a pre-determined level. These campaigns really shine when tied to an awareness initiative, as featured in the example below.

What You Need   A presence on a location-based platform, an engaging campaign or event, a cause-marketing partner or donor willing to fund the donation, and a physical location where users can check in

How to Do It
1. Decide which platform you would like to run the campaign on—foursquare and Gowalla are both good choices.
2. Determine the goal of your campaign (and your partner). Do you want to raise awareness of an issue or are you simply adding a philanthropic layer to an existing event where people will be checking in?
3. Determine the target gift amount and the donation increments for check ins. If your partner is willing to donate $1000, then set a realistic goal for how many people will check in, divide it in half (to be safe), and then divide the target gift amount by that number (i.e., if you think 200 people will check in, cut it in half to get to 100 and make each check in worth $10, maxing out at $1000).
4. Set up the check-in point on your preferred platform.
5. Publicize the campaign via any and all marketing vehicles. Be sure to post instructions very clearly at the check-in location (i.e., "Check-in at the Museum store and Museumworks will donate $10 to our organization!").

A Closer Look   In 2010, in an effort to raise awareness of environmental issues and to raise some much-needed funds to advocate for them, Earthjustice launched a check in for charity campaign.

Earthjustice (www.earthjustice.org) is a nonprofit public interest law firm dedicated to protecting the magnificent places, natural resources, and wildlife of this earth, and to defending the right of all people to a healthy environment.

The organization placed posters in San Francisco BART stations
and each time a user checked in at a designated ad, an unnamed
major donor gave $10 to help the organization's attorneys protect
the environment. The call to action on one of the ads was "Use
Your Cell Phone to Drill the Oil Industry," intended to raise awareness of unsafe oil drilling. In the fine print, the ad stated that
the donations were limited to one check in per user, per day
and the total gift maxed out at $50,000. This was a brilliant way to
engage a younger, tech-savvy crowd in a very well-trafficked area.

According to Ray Wan, Earthjustice's marketing manager, the
"drill the oil industry ad" was done right after the BP oil spill to
capitalize on public anger and concern about unsafe oil drilling
practices (see Exhibit 4.4). Other ads focused on targeted issues
that were important to the San Francisco community (protecting
Lake Tahoe and California endangered species).

"We asked folks to check in on foursquare rather than go to a
URL because of how fast and easy it was to check in versus typing in

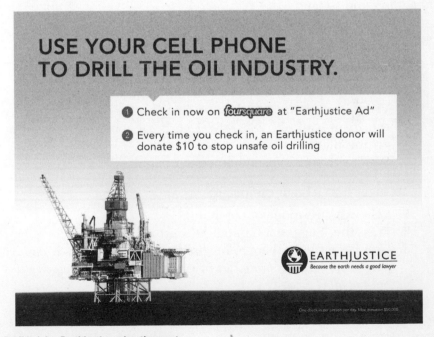

Exhibit 4.4   Earthjustice advertisement
Source: Courtesy of Earthjustice/earthjustice.org

a URL, filling out an online form, etc.," says Ray. "This dramatically increased the rate of participation."

 Participate in Social Buying Platforms

Social buying platforms like Groupon and LivingSocial offer your nonprofit the unique opportunity to get in front a huge audience and attract hundreds of new supporters. The beauty in these platforms is the ability to do low-cost acquisition and the potential to grow your supporter base. Nonprofits can either opt to participate in a daily deal, offering a discounted rate on their services or attractions, or in select cities, participate in Groupon's G-Team campaigns, which are designed to benefit the local communities of subscribers.

What You Need   An offer: tickets, membership, matching gifts, merchandise, and so on

How to Do It

To submit a daily deal:

1. Select the platform. For this example, we will use Groupon.
2. Visit www.grouponworks.com/get-featured and complete the form, call 877.788.7858 Ext. 2, or e-mail advertising@groupon.com.
3. Work with your representative to formulate an offer.

To suggest a G-Team campaign:

1. Visit www.groupon.com/g-team.
2. Press the "Suggest a Campaign" button.
3. Complete the G-Team Sponsorship Application. *G-Team campaigns are currently being run in many of the major Groupon cities, but not all of them.*

A Closer Look   Some criticize discounting memberships or tickets, so it depends on your organization's philosophy, but if you are looking to increase traffic and exposure to your organization, this is a sure way to do it. There are many ways that nonprofits are leveraging the power of collective buying to further their cause:

- Save The Children secured a $225,000 matching gift and funded a Groupon daily deal with it. If Groupon users made a $15 donation, it would automatically be doubled. 1953 people purchased the Groupon, earning Save The Children nearly $60,000.
- LivingSocial funded a similar fundraising campaign for the American Red Cross Japan Earthquake and Pacific Tsunami Fund. For every $5 gift from a LivingSocial user, the company donated $5. The total of all the donations and the match was $2,162,570.
- The Charleston Museum offered up discounted one-year memberships for its daily deal on Groupon. With three levels to choose from, the organization sold 352 memberships. And, with nine out of ten businesses using Groupon seeing an increase in repeat customers, that is quite an acquisition tool.
- The Boston Dogs Organization offered an hour-long, in-home session with a dog trainer for its LivingSocial deal. Seventy-seven sessions were purchased.
- Through a G-Team campaign, Lights. Camera. Help! (a non-profit that trains other nonprofits on video across the United States) offered a video workshop for five Austin nonprofits if the deal reached the tipping point at $1000 in donations. It did and buyers received "100 percent off free, priceless karma."

 ## Submit Your Organization to be Featured on Philanthroper

Based on the oh-so-popular "daily deals" models of group-buying sites like Groupon and LivingSocial, Philanthroper gathers donations for one nonprofit per day. The site features the story of a new 501(c)3 nonprofit each day and readers have an option to give $1 to $10 to the organization via their PayPal accounts. Philanthroper borrows from location-based giants foursquare and Gowalla by providing profile pages with virtual incentives, or medals, to reward users for their philanthropic progress. Just as with the daily deal sites, users can share news of their donation on Facebook or "Tweet the Cause" to their followers. This is a new and growing site to watch.

What You Need   A 501(c)3 designation (Philanthroper does not promote religious-oriented nonprofits)

How to Do It   E-mail tips@philanthroper.com to suggest an organization. (Although it will feature larger nonprofits, Philanthroper focuses on young and growing nonprofits bringing in less than $1 million a year in revenue.)

A Closer Look   When the USO was featured on Philanthroper, $319 was raised. What may seem like a small donation to some was very valuable and quantifiable for the organization's "Operation Phone Home" program.

"Ask any USO volunteer what most troops look for when they walk through the door, and it's the phone. They walk in, they grab a phone, and call home," says Gena Fitzgerald, USO's vice president of communications. "Getting a call from someone you love and knowing that they are okay is like nothing else in the world."

Operation Phone Home is a program of the USO that provides and distributes international, prepaid calling cards to servicemen and women across the globe. With the $319 that the organization received, it was able to provide nearly 100 hours of talk time to soldiers phoning home—and that is priceless.

"By using the retail space and successful publishing practices as our models, we're building what I really believe is the first nonprofit site that appeals to general consumers rather than just donors," says Mark Wilson, founder of Philanthroper.com. "I think we'll see Generation Y giving less money to more causes more

The United Service Organizations (USO; www.uso.org) lifts the spirits of America's troops and their families.

quickly than before, so we built a platform customized for fast, bite-sized content."

 ## 88 Ask Supporters to Pledge Social Actions

Social media generates an endless supply of digital activity, and these actions can be turned into donations using services like HelpAttack! by asking your supporters to pledge their social actions. Pledging is one of the most tried and true ways to collect donations, and HelpAttack! can help turn Twitter and Facebook updates into real money. Converting online activity into real change is the goal, and the low barrier to entry for pledging is a great way to get your social audience to take a first step towards becoming donors.

What You Need   An account at HelpAttack!

How to Do It
1. Visit HelpAttack.com and press the "Add Your Cause or Nonprofit" button.
2. Enter your organization's information.
3. Create a communications strategy to tell your supporters about the social pledging campaign.
4. Promote the campaign and monitor the results.

A Closer Look   Social pledging is a fun, new way for supporters to give, and builds on one of the oldest nonprofit fundraising methods: the pledge. David J. Neff, author and co-founder of HelpAttack!, says, "Nonprofits of all sizes and shapes have relied on pledges for years. Pledges based on stocks sold, events held, or even pledges to pay at the end of an auction. What we are doing is modernizing that for the world of social media and making it fun by rewarding their pledges with coins and competing against their friends."

In March of 2011, Best Friends Animal Society (BFAS) launched a campaign targeting its Twitter and Facebook followers. Five social updates were made asking supporters to pledge their social updates using the HelpAttack! platform (see Exhibit 4.5).

Exhibit 4.5   Best Friends Animal Society HelpAttack! page
Source: Courtesy of Best Friends Animal Society; HelpAttack!

The BFAS supporters responded positively, pledging and sharing the campaign with their own networks.

By the end of April, more than 64 people had pledged their social updates to BFAS. To date, more than $1,400 of these pledges have been collected, making it clear that social supporters were willing to step up and help a cause they cared about.

Raising money using social pledging will work best if you have an active and engaged following on Facebook and Twitter, but it's certainly worth a try. Social media fundraising is still new to many people, and that alone may be enough to get them to pledge.

 Participate in Social Gaming

Playing games is one of the world's best diversions, and the emotional attachment people have to social gaming can drive them to take action for your organization, including making a donation. By taking advantage of social platforms like Facebook, in-game activity spreads through personal networks, increasing the reach of your nonprofit's message. By partnering with companies like Zynga, virtual goods can even be bought by players, which delivers money directly to your cause.

What You Need   A campaign or cause that will attract a gaming demographic, and budget to create a game

How to Do It
1. Identify an audience for your game that will maximize both playing time and propensity to donate.
2. Create a campaign to tie a game into, and decide what platform the game should live on (e.g., web site, Facebook, smartphone).
3. Develop a game internally, with an interactive agency, or by partnering with an existing game platform.
4. Promote the game and campaign together by communicating with your target audience. Encourage participants to share the game both via the marketing materials and with in-game features.

A Closer Look   Taking the plunge into social gaming can be a big commitment even for a large nonprofit, but there are no signs that the industry is slowing down. According to eMarketer, marketers will spend \$293 million on in-game advertisements in 2011,[9] which presents nonprofits with a lot of partnership opportunities. Zynga makes many of the most popular social games with more than 215 million monthly players,[10] and its games can be played by all of Facebook's 500 million users.[11] Clearly, the numbers are there.

Zynga is the company behind FarmVille, one of the most popular social games of all time, and it often partners with nonprofits seeking to raise money through one of its platforms. Players can purchase limited edition items inside games, and the proceeds

---

[9]Clark Fredricksen, "Marketers to Spend \$220 Million on Advertisements in Social Games This Year," eMarketer, August 11, 2010, www.emarketer.com/blog/index .php/marketers-spend-220-million-advertisements-social-games-year.
[10]"Fact Sheet," Zynga, http://company.zynga.com/about/press/fact-sheet.
[11]"Statistics," Facebook, http://www.facebook.com/press/info.php?statistics.

go directly to participating nonprofits. Zynga and its games have helped raise a lot of money for Haiti-based initiatives that support earthquake recovery.

Partnering with a company like Zynga is one way to use social gaming, but stand-alone games can be created, too. A successful social game starts with a great idea, so be sure to explore the many cause-focused games that have already been created. Visit Gamesforchange.org and take a look around its "Play" section, where the organization curates social games from around the world. Here you will find many different game concepts and platforms that can help you get ideas for your own game.

 Take your Fundraising Events to an Alternate Reality

Virtual events are a great way to engage supporters without the boundaries of geographic borders or physical limitations. Whether you choose to run an event on your web site, or within a virtual world like Second Life, a virtual event or a virtual component of an event can greatly extend your real-world fundraising. Plus, virtual events have a much lower cost to produce than their real-world counterparts, increasing fundraising efficiency.

What You Need   Since this is a particularly advanced tactic, let's start with the basics by establishing a presence in Second Life and exploring the resources available to nonprofits

How to Do It
1. Sign up for a free membership at Secondlife.com, create your avatar, and start exploring.
2. Visit Nonprofitcommons.org, an educational outreach program of TechSoup Global that was designed to lower the barriers of access to Second Life, to create a community of practice for nonprofits to explore and learn about the virtual world, and to investigate the many ways in which nonprofits might utilize this unique environment. Techsoup Global hosts weekly meetings in the Nonprofit Commons Amphitheater, every Friday at 8:30 a.m. PST. Once you create an avatar at Secondlife.com and identify yourself as a nonprofit, you

will be teleported to the Nonprofit Commons Archipelago, where you will be provided with everything you need to get started on your journey.

3. If establishing a presence for your nonprofit fits in with your social-media strategy, a great place to start is by setting up a free office space through Nonprofit Commons where you can network with other nonprofits in Second Life and learn about how they are leveraging the virtual world.

A Closer Look

The American Cancer Society (www.cancer.org) is the nationwide, community-based, voluntary health organization dedicated to eliminating cancer as a major health problem by preventing cancer, saving lives, and diminishing suffering from cancer, through research, education, advocacy, and service.

In 2005, the American Cancer Society took its signature fundraising event, Relay For Life, three dimensional in the virtual world Second Life. Relay for Life of Second Life (RFLofSL) takes place annually in July with volunteers forming or joining teams starting in mid-March.

Just as in the real event, virtual participants fundraise, walk a track, and camp out at the event. The first RFLofSL took place in August 2005, raising $5,000 with 315 "avatars" or virtual participants. The event continued to grow and in 2010, the sixth RFLofSL took place in July raising $222,804 with 1,579 avatars participating, walking 2,676 laps around the virtual track.[12] Since 2005, the American Cancer Society has raised more than $950,000 in Second Life.[13]

Supporters can donate using their credit card at RelayForLife .org/SecondLife or their "Linden dollars" (the currency in Second Life that translates into real dollars) at RFLofSL kiosks, with team vendor cards, or through virtual luminaries at the event.

---

[12]"Relay for Life of Second Life," Relay for Life, www.cancer.org/Involved/ Participate/RelayForLife/second-life.
[13]"Relay For Life of Second Life," Second Life Wiki, updated May 6, 2011, http://wiki.secondlife.com/wiki/Relay_For_Life_of_Second_Life.

"Any organization, no matter how small or how little their budget is, can benefit from this social networking space," says Susan Tenby, Online Community Director, TechSoup.org and Nonprofit Commons in Second Life. "And not to forget, awareness in the virtual world often translates into actual real-world donations."

5

Measure

Smart nonprofit executives and managers keep an eye on the return on investment (ROI) of all organizational activity, including marketing communications and social media. So whether you're measuring a return on investment, interaction, or impact, collecting meaningful data is critical to understanding the effectiveness of your social media program.

Social media provides new ways of understanding nonprofit supporters, and it's up to interactive managers to mine this data for useful information. Knowing the gender and age of your Facebook followers can tell you a lot, and hearing what the general public is saying about you on Twitter may tell you even more. You can even find out when people stop watching your YouTube videos! Explore these data sets, and find the metrics that help show that your social media efforts are meeting organizational goals.

Because the measurement and tracking of social media is still a discipline in development, there is no silver bullet when deciding what data your organization should be capturing. Focusing on metrics and key performance indicators that tie in with your overall organizational goals is a good place to start. If you're trying to reach a younger audience, look at Facebook demographic data. If you need to increase awareness of your mission, measure the impressions and overall reach of your content.

If you're just getting started with social media, the tactics in this chapter will introduce you to some of the key platforms and methodologies used to measure social interaction. If you have an established program, these tactics will help you fill in holes and learn to track new types of data. Either way, you'll learn that measuring your social-media activity is important toward understanding how this powerful platform is shaping your supporters' interactions.

 Analyze Facebook Activity with Insights

Facebook has become an effective place to engage your supporters, so understanding who they are and how they interact with your content is critical to sustained success on the platform. Facebook Insights provides free analytics for page administrators that can be used to determine which updates resonate with your fans, as well as valuable demographic information on your visitors. Using Facebook Insights to better understand your supporters and content will help you do a better job using the platform to meet your mission.

What You Need   A Facebook page

How to Do It

1. Visit your organization's Facebook page (you must have admin rights to view Insights).
2. Click the "View Insights" link in the "Admins" panel located in the upper right.
3. View high-level statistics for your page, and change the data range as needed.
4. Click "Users" in the left navigation to see details about your Facebook fans. Here you can see activity level and demographic information (e.g., age and gender).
5. Click "Interactions" to see how each piece of content is performing. This will show the total impressions and interaction level for each item you post on your organization's wall.
6. Export key metrics to a spreadsheet if you are using one.

A Closer Look   For most nonprofits, posting content to Facebook has become second nature. Because of this, it's important that Insights are used to ensure that all of that activity is having a positive effect on your mission. Insights will help you determine if updates are being seen, if your target audience is who you thought it was, and if your page is healthy.

Like with any analytics program (e.g., Google Analytics), there is a lot of data to consume—don't get overwhelmed! Find metrics that make sense for you and your organization's goals. If you are trying to reach younger supporters, pay attention to the demographic data. If you want to increase the readership of your blog, take a hard look at the interactions of each wall update.

Here are a few key areas that every nonprofit should be looking at in Facebook Insights:

- Demographics—Being able to see age, gender, location, and language details is one of the best things about Facebook Insights. Don't miss this opportunity to create profiles of your average Facebook fans, which will help you better target them in the future.
- External Referrers—Found on the "Users" page, this helpful list will tell you how people are finding your page.
- Daily Story Feedback—This data set is on the "Interactions" page, and will show you what fans like to do on your page (e.g., like a post, leave a comment).
- Page Posts—Also on the "Interactions Page", this table will show you each wall update's impressions and feedback. Sorting this data by feedback percentage will show you which wall updates your fans respond to.
- Total Tab Views—If you've built custom tabs, this data set will show you how each one is performing.

92 Understand Your YouTube Audience

Knowing your audience, and their behavior, is key to understanding what video content will work for your organization. YouTube's Insight platform is a data-rich window into your viewers' activity, and can tell you exactly how your video content is performing. Use Insight to see how often videos are watched, who is watching, how they are watching, and whether they are engaging with the content. Hot Spots even show when audience attention peaks and drops off, so you can make your next videos even more compelling.

What You Need A YouTube account and videos to upload

How to Do It

1. Create a YouTube account and channel.
2. Upload videos and feature them on your web site, blog, and Facebook page.
3. Visit your "My Videos" page and click the "Insight" tab. This will load the data for your entire channel.
4. To access metrics on individual videos, click the "Insight stats" link on each video's page, or press the "Insight" button below each video on the "My Videos" page.
5. Collect key stats and put them into a spreadsheet, database, or other external location you are using to save social media metrics.

A Closer Look   Like any metrics program, YouTube's Insight provides a bunch of numbers that will help you understand who your audience is and what content they like to consume. On their own, these numbers don't mean much—but if you monitor them over time, you'll notice helpful patterns emerge. You'll see who your target audience is and why (or why they aren't) watching your favorite videos.

Getting a high-level view of your YouTube audience is important, but you really want to understand how each video is performing in order to create better content in the future. At the video level, here are some key areas of Insight you need to be paying attention to:

- Data Range—This section is always visible and defaults to one week in duration, so be sure to expand it to see how each video performed over time.
- Views—You can see how popular each video is in this section, with the ability to drill down into geography and unique visitors.
- Discovery—This section will show how viewers found each video, whether from your YouTube channel, a YouTube search, or an external web site. It also shows how the YouTube player was being used when the video was viewed.
- Demographics—Any social program that can provide demographic information rocks, so be sure to mine Insight for all you can about your audience. Here, you can see the gender and age breakdown of people watching each video.

- Community—This section shows how engaged your audience is with each video, including shares, comments, ratings, and favorites.
- Hot Spots—Possibly the most useful section of Insight, Hot Spots measures the audience attention level compared to similar videos, and will show you exactly when viewers stopped watching each video.

93 Track Referrals from Social Sites

Tracking the number of visitors your web site receives from social media channels is a critical metric needed to understand the effectiveness of your social marketing program. Many social media managers have goals around increasing traffic to their organization's web sites and blogs, and social activity often results in referrals from Facebook, Twitter, LinkedIn, and so on. Referrals are great for showing the health of social marketing efforts, and they can tell which platform is sending you the most visitors.

What You Need   A web site or blog, a web analytics tool, and social media accounts

How to Do It
1. Post links to blog posts and Web pages on social sites (e.g., Facebook, Twitter, StumbleUpon).
2. Open up your web analytics tool (this example uses Google Analytics), and select a long enough data range to show good information. It's often good to compare a range to the past, so you can see year-over-year growth.
3. Click "Traffic Sources" in the left navigation.
4. Click "Referring Sites" in the left navigation.
5. The Referring Sites page displays the top 10 web sites sending you visitors. Use the "Show rows:" drop-down menu in the lower right to increase the range.
6. Look for social web sites in the list (e.g., Facebook.com, Twitter.com, LinkedIn.com, StumbleUpon.com).

7. Drill into each social source by clicking its name, which should be a link. This will show you the spikes in traffic for each platform, so you can correlate it with certain activities.

A Closer Look   Increasing traffic to your organization's web site and blog is likely an important goal for you, so understanding your referral traffic's impact from social sites is critical. Measuring the number of visits each social network generates for your web site can help show ROI, especially if you know how many visitors your site converts into donors, volunteers, or members.

Some good ways to use referral data include:

- Measure the referral rank of each social site, and watch how it changes over time. Facebook may be sixteenth on the list one year, then eleventh on the list the next year. StumbleUpon may not even be on the list, but after seeding the site with some of your content it may move up to the top 10.
- Measure traffic spikes from a single network, and match each increase with a particular social activity. For instance, you may have hosted a contest on Facebook (see Tactic 65). If you think a lot of visitors came to your web site because of the contest, use referrals to prove this!
- Look at the behavior of the referral traffic from each site. You can determine if Facebook users visit more pages on your web site than LinkedIn users, or how many visitors from social sites are new (see Tactic 94).
- In addition to using a web analytics program, consistently using a short URL service like bit.ly (see Tactic 95) will provide a good view of your social referrals. Using the same bit.ly link on Facebook, Twitter, and blogs will allow you to measure clicks and user information. While this doesn't provide as deep of a dive as Google Analytics, this is a quick and easy way to measure how many clicks you're getting from your social channel.

94   Measure New Visitors from Social Channels

A successful social media program does many things, and generating awareness and interest in your organization should be at the top of the list. Monitoring new visitors to your organization's web site or blog is a great way to measure awareness, especially among people who are new to your mission. Measuring new visitors to your web site will give you a sense of how many non-financial supporters your social program is generating, which will help fill your donor pipeline in the future.

What You Need   A web site or blog, a web analytics tool, and social media accounts

How to Do It
1. Post links to blog posts and web pages on social sites (e.g., Facebook, Twitter, StumbleUpon).
2. Open up your web analytics program and navigate to the referrals section. If you're using Google Analytics, click "Traffic Sources" then "Site Referrals" in the left navigation.
3. Find a social site in the report's list that your organization is using, such as Facebook.com or Twitter.com, and click its name (which should be a link). If you don't see the network you're looking for, expand the rows of the report.
4. In the Site Usage row, look for the "% New Visits" section. This will show the percentage of visitors who are new to your web site and compare that number to the site's average.
5. Change the data range field and look for spikes caused by events or campaigns, and look for overall trends (such as increasing new visitors over time).

A Closer Look   New visitors are important to your web site and blog because they indicate an awareness and interest in your organization. Whether the visits are coming from Google, direct mail, Facebook, or Twitter, these visitors could be next year's donors—so make sure your pipeline of new visitors remains full. Social media can help with that.

A web analytics program is the easiest way to measure new visitors, who are people who have never visited your web site before. Visits from Facebook, Twitter, LinkedIn, and so on, can be easily seen and measured at a granular level, including percentage of new visits. This percentage of new visitors is key, as it will help you understand the type of traffic that social channels are sending to your web site.

Look at the percentage of new visitors on its own, but also compared to the rest of your web site. Ideally, social networks should be sending a lot of new visitors to your web site. But be sure to look at the total number of visits, not just the percentage—70 percent of 100 is different than 70 percent of 10,000. Just because you have a high percentage of new visitors coming from Twitter .com, that doesn't mean it's a high number—you have to measure to be sure!

 ## Track Link Performance with Short URLs

Social media is an important channel to use when linking to your organization's online content, so it's critical to track how each link performs. Short URL services like bit.ly and goo.gl create small links that can be used in the 140-character-or-less world of Twitter. Once a short URL is clicked in a tweet, Facebook update, or blog post, the data is captured and can be analyzed in real time. Seeing how many people clicked a link, where they were from, and what platform they were using provides a big picture view of how your content moves through the social sphere.

What You Need   A Twitter account and a bit.ly account

How to Do It
1. Visit bit.ly and create an account. Having an account will make it easier to manage and measure your short URLs.
2. Copy the URL you want to shorten, and paste it into the bit.ly "Shorten your links and share from here" field.
3. Copy the short URL that has been created, and paste it in your next tweet, Facebook update, or blog post.
4. Visit the info page for the bit.ly URL and check out the statistics. The info page can be reached by clicking the "Info Page+" link on your bit.ly home page or by simply adding a plus sign at the end of any bit.ly URL.

A Closer Look   Using short URLs has become a standard practice for social media managers. What started out as a way to put long links into short Twitter updates has turned into a full-fledged link-tracking process. It's common to now see bit.ly links used across many social platforms, including Facebook, LinkedIn, blogs, and e-mail, with integration in desktop clients like Tweetdeck.

If content is going to be shared by multiple staff members and an army of supporters, having a single, short URL will make tracking much easier. Because of this, social media managers often turn to services like bit.ly to manage the process. Here are some useful details about the bit.ly platform:

- The URL's info page is where all the important data lives, even though you can see total number of clicks from your account's home page. To get to the info page, just add a plus sign to the end of any bit.ly URL. You can also click the "Info Page+" link on the home page of your account.
- Bit.ly will tell you if another user has created a short URL pointing to the same web content, and provides the aggregate number of clicks it has received. This is a great way to gauge the popularity of your content, as well as get some data on that activity.
- Quick Response Codes, or QR Codes, are a fun way to put calls to action on paper (see Tactic 44). Every bit.ly URL automatically generates a QR code, and this can be downloaded from the short URL's info page.
- The info page also shows conversation data consisting of mentions on Twitter and Facebook. Seeing the number of shares, links, and comments can help you measure the engagement of content.
- Additional metrics around referrer details and geographic location provide a snapshot of where people are clicking on your links.

96   Monitor Your Organization's Name on Twitter

Keeping an eye on who is talking about your organization on Twitter is a great place to start with social media, and over time will become a necessary tool if you want to engage with your supporters in real time. By using Twitter's own search tool, it's easy to track mentions of your organization's name, programs, campaigns, and key staff members who have a public profile. Seeing what is being said about your organization will help you better understand your social audience, react in real time, and improve your mission delivery.

What You Need   A Twitter account and a tool to monitor Twitter searches

How to Do It
1. Determine what aspects of your organization should be monitored. These include your organization's name, Twitter handle, executive director, campaign names, program names, and so on.
2. Visit search.twitter.com and type in these keywords and phrases to see what is being said.
3. Locate the "Feed for this Query" link in the upper right portion of the search results screen.
4. Copy the URLs for each feed you want to monitor in real time.
5. Input these feed URLs into a RSS reader, or build a listening dashboard in iGoogle (see Tactic 99). If you are using a tool like Tweetdeck, these search terms can be set up as columns.

A Closer Look   Before search.twitter.com, nonprofits had a difficult time getting instant feedback from their supporters. With today's social monitoring tools, nonprofits can immediately see how people feel about their organizations, programs, and campaigns—especially on Twitter.

Social media managers need to use the power of Search.twitter. com to monitor everything, not just their organization's name—though that's a great place to start. Here are some things you should be listening for on Twitter:

- Organization Name—Look for mentions of your organization's name, including full name, acronyms, and abbreviations.
- Names of Public Figures—If you have a visible executive director, vocal board member, or popular volunteer coordinator, search for their names on Twitter.
- Program Names—Search for key program names that are popular with your supporters.

- Campaign Names—As with programs, campaign names can be searched to reveal chatter.
- Twitter Accounts—Do searches on organizational Twitter accounts, including your main handle, local branches, events, and program accounts.
- Locations—If your mission serves a local area, city, town, or even neighborhood, search Twitter to monitor general chatter—you might learn a lot about your community.

Once you perform a search for these terms, you can grab the RSS feed and place it in a reader or an iGoogle dashboard. You can also set up your Twitter client, like TweetDeck and Seesmic, to monitor these terms in real time.

 ## Measure the Reach of Your Tweets

If your nonprofit is using Twitter to raise awareness, advocate for a cause, or engage a community, you'll want to ensure that each message is reaching as many people as possible. Services like Tweet Reach.com help determine how far your organization's tweets travel. The total impressions of your Twitter account and particular tweets can be analyzed, as well as impressions generated by other Twitter users on your behalf. These metrics are a great way to measure the impact of your Twitter activity.

What You Need   A Twitter account

How to Do It
1. Identify a Twitter account, hashtag, or tweet you want to measure.
2. Visit www.tweetreach.com.
3. Enter your terms into the search field, and press the "Go" button.
4. Look at the total reach, impressions, and types of tweets for your terms.
5. Note which Twitter users helped spread the message, as these accounts can be considered key influencers.
6. Record these numbers in an external document for future benchmarking.

A Closer Look Measuring the reach of your tweets is important to understanding how your Twitter activity is making an impact on your marketing communications. From an impression-based view of marketing, reach is a key component when looking at the ROI of social media. Impressions are used to measure the success of pay-per-click campaigns, e-mail blasts, and web site activity, and social media is no different. Being able to report on social media impressions at a campaign level will help nonprofit executives understand the impact of Twitter.

Using services like TweetReach.com will help establish a baseline measurement for the reach of your Twitter activity. By measuring weekly, or even daily, you can look at the data and patterns to see how different content affects the reach of your tweets, and which influencers are sharing your message.

Putting an actual number on how far your messages are traveling will help you maximize the impact of each future tweet. Measuring reach will tell you which hashtags get the most impressions, and which Twitter users have the biggest influence (Exhibit 5.1). Using this information, you can craft tweets that will reach the largest audience.

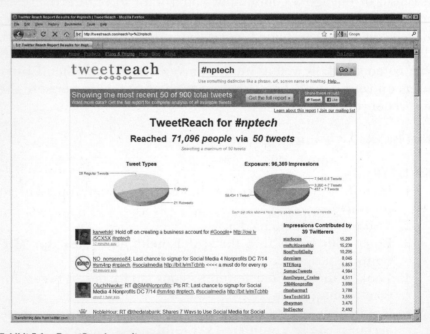

Exhibit 5.1   TweetReach results page
Source: Courtesy of TweetReach

To take a deeper dive into the data, TweetReach.com has a few additional options. If understanding your organization's digital influence is a key factor of your social program, TweetReach.com offers paid plans that include trackers, reports, and multiple user support.

 ## Calculate Your Twitter Influence

If you're using Twitter, understanding the influence and impact of your tweets will help you be more successful. If your influence goes up, your message is likely being heard and acted upon. If your influence is going down, you're likely reaching out to the wrong people about the wrong topics. Thankfully, tools like Klout.com can actually measure the influence of your Twitter account, providing a useful metric that can help your organization's Twitter activity be more effective.

What You Need   A Twitter account and some followers

How to Do It

1. Visit www.klout.com and press the "Sign In with Twitter" button.
2. Check out your "Klout Score" in the upper left—you can't miss it!
3. Note the numbers and names of people that your account influences, as well as what topics you are influential about.
4. Scroll through the "Score Analysis" tab, and look at your score, network influence, amplification probability, and true reach.
5. Click the "Topics" tab to see the subject matter you are influential on.
6. Click the "Influencers" tab for a breakdown of Twitter users who are influenced by you, and what type of Twitter users they are.

A Closer Look   Measuring the influence of your organization's Twitter account is just as important as identifying your top Twitter followers for the same reason—reputation matters! You want your organization's Twitter feed to be a critical, meaningful source of information for your supporters. Measuring influence with Klout. com will give you a set of metrics to measure that.

The Klout Score is created using a host of individual metrics, which means Klout.com can slice up social data in many different ways. Be sure to look around to find metrics that capture key information about the success of your social media program. Here are a few key areas of Klout.com and what they measure:

- The Klout Score—This number represents the overall influence of your Twitter account. This number is a good benchmark to monitor as you move forward.
- True Reach—This metric looks at the size of your engaged audience, will tell you if your tweets are good at building audience, and show how far your tweets travel. True Reach also looks at demand, which is based on how many accounts you had to follow to get your own followers.
- Amplification Probability—This is the likelihood that your content will be retweeted, generate a conversation, and lead to other actions.
- Network Influence—This is the influence level of your engaged audience. This metric can tell you how influential the Twitter users you interact with are.

Get to know your reputation, and monitor how it changes so you can be more effective in the future. You need to know your audience, but you need to know yourself too!

 Create a Social Media Listening Dashboard

Social media has proven to be a must-have tool for communication and engagement, but turning the megaphone around and listening to the chatter is yet another way to use it effectively. Supporters are tweeting, blogging, commenting, and mentioning nonprofits every day, and social media search tools can be used to find and monitor these conversations. By utilizing RSS feeds using iGoogle, you can create a listening dashboard that can be shared across your entire organization.

What You Need A Facebook page, a Twitter account, and a shared Google account

How to Do It

1. Determine what names, terms, and keywords you want to monitor. These should include your organization's name, key staff members, program names, campaign names, local keywords, and hashtags.
2. Visit online social services and search for the terms you identified in step 1. Perform the search and copy the RSS feed for each result if one is available.
3. Use search.twitter.com to capture what people are saying on Twitter.
4. Use www.socialmention.com to capture what people are saying on various social channels.
5. Use www.icerocket.com to capture what people are saying on blogs.
6. Use www.boardreader.com to capture what people are saying on discussion forums.
7. Use www.google.com/alerts to capture what people are saying on web sites. Create each Google Alert to be delivered by feed, then copy the RSS feed URL for each alert.
8. Log in to a Google account and access iGoogle by visiting www.google.com/ig. Placing multiple iGoogle RSS gadgets on a single page will create a dashboard.
9. Click the "Add Gadgets" link in the upper right portion of the screen.
10. Click the "Add feed or gadget" link at the bottom of the left column.
11. Paste in one of the feed URLs you created in steps 2 through 6, and press the "Add" button.
12. Click the close button, and continue to add as many feeds as you need.
13. Visit your iGoogle home page and confirm the RSS gadgets are displaying. You can reposition them by dragging them around the page.

A Closer Look Creating a social media listening dashboard (Exhibit 5.2) is one of the first things that should be done when creating a program from scratch. Having a single screen that displays the social

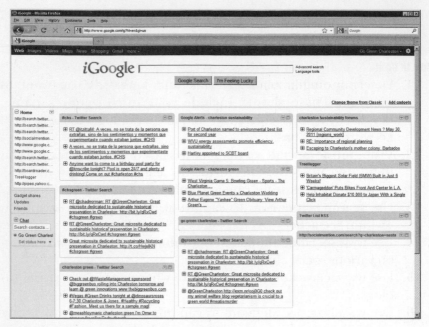

Exhibit 5.2   Go Green Charleston iGoogle dashboard

Source: Courtesy of Go Green Charleston; Google

chatter about your organization is an effective way to monitor these conversations, allowing you to see what's being discussed and respond promptly.

A dashboard made in iGoogle is also a great way to share this goldmine of social feedback with the rest of your organization, allowing them to see social conversations in real time. Sharing a social dashboard with an executive director who isn't sold on social media will really open his or her eyes.

Social dashboards like these are only as strong as their supporting RSS feeds, so find feeds that contain good information for your organization. Here are a few ways you can listen to each social network:

- Twitter—Use Search.twitter.com for some of the best real-time information. You can also include search columns for key terms in Twitter clients, like Tweetdeck.
- Facebook—Open up your organization's wall (see Tactic 9) and pay close attention. You can also view public comments on your Community Page if you have one.

- Blogs—Search sites like www.icerocket.com and www.technorati.com to capture much of what is being said about your organization on blogs. Google Alerts will catch a lot, too.
- Discussion Forums—Use services like www.boardreader.com and www.omgili.com to find mentions of your organization on discussion forums and boards.
- Social News—Search each news site and add the results to your dashboard if they have an RSS feed. This includes www.digg.com, www.stumbleupon.com, www.reddit.com, and so on.
- LinkedIn—The search functionality at LinkedIn.com allows you to save searches, and you can also use www.socialmention.com to see activity from the network.
- Web sites—Setup Google Alerts to catch any mentions of your organization on web sites and blogs.

 Use Social Media Monitoring Applications

While there are many free tools to monitor your brand, engage with your various social networks, and measure results, there are an increasing number of paid services that pull it all together. Just as with any other software application, you get out of it what you put into it, so unless you are fully staffed on the social media front, we suggest adding the full-featured platform to your "social media wish list." There is a tipping point at which it makes sense to invest in it, but not when social media is just one part of one person's job. There are several lighter-weight applications that you may wish to opt for instead that charge a small monthly fee.

What You Need A full-time social media manager, a technology budget of anywhere from $300 to more than $5000 a year, and keywords for search

How to Do It Determine what your organization's needs and budget are, and evaluate multiple systems.

A Closer Look Many premium services of otherwise free tools offer very affordable upgrades that include basic analytics, while there are also full-featured platforms that handle every aspect of social media from listening to reporting. Nonprofit social media strategist JD Lasica, who runs Socialbrite.org, a great resource with thousands of free articles and resources for nonprofits, shares his top picks for subscription-based social media monitoring tools to consider when evaluating your monitoring needs:

- Sprout Social (http://sproutsocial.com) lets you target and discover new customers or supporters, monitor your brand across the social Web, organize your social networks, and manage up to five identities with the basic plan. The service offers an easy-to-digest summary of what's happening online around your social presence. The Pro Plan at $9 per month is geared to nonprofits, with a free trial.
- Trackur (www.trackur.com) is an online reputation management and social media-monitoring tool created by a team of reputation experts. Think of it as Google Alerts on steroids. Trackur will rate the clout of your online influencers so you can easily interact with them, and it delivers results to your e-mail inbox, RSS feed, or web-based dashboard. Quickly monitor your reputation, check on trends, and analyze media mentions for your nonprofit, brand, sector, or cause. They have more than 27,000 users and, at last word, offer plans starting at $18 per month, with a free 10-day money-back guarantee.
- uberVU (www.uberVU.com) is a social media-monitoring tool that combines ease of use with powerful features such as historical and real-time data and "sentiment analysis," a fancy way of saying they look at whether people are saying nice or bad things about you. Packages start at $499 per month for individuals with a 14-day free trial.
- Thrive, from the consultancy Small Act of McLean, Virginia (www.smallact.com), is an all-in-one social media tool that lets you listen, publish, report, and engage with donors and supporters. Features like contact tagging and sorting, automated keyword searching, and automated conversation archiving help you cultivate relationships over time, turning fans into donors. Import your existing e-mail lists and convert them into detailed social profiles so you can jump-start your social media program. The recommended plan for most nonprofits is $99 per month per user.

101   Get a Strategy

Okay, so getting a social strategy isn't really a tactic—you caught us. If you've read this far, you've certainly picked up a few ideas for your social media program and are anxious to get started. But before you go implement them, make sure each tactic will produce the results needed to meet your marketing, fundraising, and organizational goals. Social media activity takes time, talent, and sometimes treasure to produce, so make sure everything you do has a real impact on your mission.

In the Introduction, we pointed you to the POST (People, Objectives, Strategy, Technology) method described in the book *Groundswell*. This is an excellent framework for creating a social media strategy that produces real results. Once a strategy is in place, you can use Tactics 1 through 100 to make it happen. Look at each desired outcome in your strategy and apply a set of tactics that will produce the results you need. Once you measure and analyze those results, it's time to refine your strategy and implement more tactics.

The fun thing about social media is that it is always changing. So, as you use this book as a guide and look to your peers for inspiration, experiment and test some new ideas with this fantastic medium that is connecting us all like never before.

About the Authors

MELANIE MATHOS has been working and volunteering with non-profits for most of her life. She now works as the senior public relations manager at Blackbaud, where she spreads the word about the company's products and services for nonprofits, co-manages its social media channels, and contributes to the NetWits ThinkTank blog. Prior to joining Blackbaud in 2006, Melanie worked as a development consultant and in the publishing industry. She also serves on the board of directors of Fields to Families, working with communications and fundraising. Melanie has a degree in journalism from Michigan State University. She lives in Charleston, South Carolina, with her husband, Gary, and their daughter, Elyse. You can follow her @melmatho.

CHAD NORMAN is an Internet strategist and interactive designer who has worked with nonprofits for his entire career. He works as the Internet marketing manager for Blackbaud, where he wrangles corporate web site content and develops social media strategy. He's the editor in chief of Blackbaud Blogs, and contributes to the NetWits ThinkTank blog. In 2007, he founded Go Green Charleston, a technology-focused nonprofit helping Charleston-area residents connect, stay informed, and mobilize around the local sustainability community. He also serves on the board of directors of Fields to Families, managing web strategy. Chad has a degree in psychology from Indiana University, and lives in Mount Pleasant, South Carolina, with his wife, Jennifer, and their children Cooper, Graham, and Zoe. You can follow him @chadnorman.

Index